Contents

Preface

This comparative study by a team of French political scientists analyses the main features of Western Europe's first transnational election campaign, and draws some conclusions for the future.

The different national perspectives and preoccupations, revealed in this study, go a long way to explain the groupings and alliances which have emerged in the first year of the European Parliament's life, and the possibilities and limits of effective action on its part.

The links between the European Parliament and the national political life of the Community's four main member-states (which were selected for analysis here because of their importance as well as their divergences) will clearly continue to show some of the characteristics reflected in these pages.

This study should provide essential guidance for all those concerned with the function of the European Parliament in the Community's political development, and with preparations for the next election in 1984.

Roger Morgan
June 1980

This study by members of the research staff of the Centre d'Etudes et de Recherches Internationales at the Fondation Nationale des Sciences Politiques, Paris, originally appeared in the *Revue Française de Science Politique,* Vol. 29, No. 6, (December 1979) under the title "Les élections européennes. Enjeux, campagnes, résultats".

I Introduction

Is the direct election of the European Parliament likely to regenerate the European Community's progress towards supranationalism, or will it, on the contrary, reinforce the trend towards inter-governmental co-operation, thus making the EEC more like a traditional international organisation? The ways in which the European election of June 1979 was organised in each of the four major countries of the Community — the drawing-up of platforms, the content of the different national campaigns, and the results of the election — provide some of the answers to this question, although they necessarily differ in some respects, since attitudes towards Europe obviously vary from one country to another.

West Germany is rightly considered one of the most European countries in the Community. Having supported the European Defence Community in the early 1950s, the Federal Republic did not subsequently oppose the initial enlargement of the European Economic Community, as France did. It is willing to consider supra-national solutions and does not oppose the idea of a possible extension of the powers of the European Assembly elected by universal suffrage.

West Germany has brought a great deal to Europe, but has also gained much from it. Having started from an unenviable position in 1949, it now plays a leading part in the Community, to the point where it evokes both admiration and fear. In West Germany, 'Europe' is now seen as an irreversible choice to which no alterna-tive solution exists. German political leaders do not feel that a reduction in power has resulted from the interdependence of the Member States of the EEC or from the numerous limitations on national sovereignty which all the States have more or less consciously accepted. The European election campaign merely confirmed existing commitments, for, with varying degrees of awareness, Germany sees its involvement in Europe as something which is truly constructive and positive. In consequence, the 'Act providing for the election of representatives to the Assembly by direct universal suffrage', a Decision taken by the EEC Council of Ministers on 20 September 1976, stirred up no controversy in West Germany; it was ratified unanimously by the Bundestag on 16 June and by the Bundesrat on 24 June, 1977.

In Italy, as in Germany, the general topic of Europe and the institutions of the Community is not a controversial one. Indeed, the whole of the political class is convinced that an Italy outside of the European framework would be doomed to Mediterranean stagnation. It is an awareness of its vulnerability and of the divisions within both the State and Italian society, just as much as the inherent difficulties of

1

its particular political and economic situation, which has always led Italy to look beyond its own borders for the guarantees and support which the country needs. The broad consensus about Europe which provides common ground both for politicians and for public opinion can also be explained by the decline of nationalist issues since the defeat of fascism, by the lesser importance of national as compared with family and regional concerns on the one hand and with international ones on the other, and finally by the widespread phenomenon of emigration, especially emigration to EEC countries, France, Germany and Belgium. There is evidence of the convergence of Italian attitudes towards Europe in the fact that the Parliament ratified the 'Brussels Act' almost unanimously on 17 February and 24 March 1977.

In France, however, the Nine's decision to proceed with the election to the European Assembly by universal suffrage was greeted with so much emotion and passion that it sometimes seemed that the application of article 138 of the Treaty of Rome might bring about a national division comparable to that which embittered French political life in the 1950s when supporters and opponents of the European Defence Community were set against one another. The debate about the European elections led to the reappearance of old arguments and unexpected alliances: many Gaullists, the Communists and the extreme right-wing nationalists spoke the same language, rejecting what they termed this 'evil scheme', and protesting against the risk of 'national dismemberment'. The Socialists stood apart from their partners in the Union of the Left and, with some reservations, accepted the principle of the elections, but a minority within the party declared that the political conditions for taking this step had not been fulfilled. Only a small group of Centrists declared their position unambiguously and defended the proposals for direct elections to the European Parliament.

There was much controversy in the months leading up to the parliamentary debate on the ratification of the Brussels agreement. The opponents of the election felt the proposal posed a serious threat to national sovereignty. In their view, the future Assembly, strengthened by its new popular legitimacy, would inevitably change its nature and become a 'supranational' authority. The danger was that such a parliament, in which France would be a minority party, might take powers away from the French National Assembly. On matters concerning vital spheres of political, economic, and social life, or on security matters, a European parliamentary majority 'with the blessing of the United States' might take decisions rather than France itself. Gaullists and Communists joined together to condemn President Giscard d'Estaing for exposing national independence to such intolerable risks. For their part, the Socialists, despite an agreement on the principle of direct elections arrived at in 1973, expressed all their criticisms of the Common Market and called for a revision of Community policy. They questioned 'the advisability of an electoral reform which would dispel neither ambiguities nor misunderstandings'. The minority within the PS expressed frank hostility to this approach which was dividing the Left and later might restrict it in carrying out its programme.

Faced with the static warfare tactics adopted by the Gaullists, the hostility of the Communists and the evasiveness of the Socialist Party, which was determined to 'leave the Right to extricate itself from its divisions', President Giscard d'Estaing proved uncompromising on the principle of the election. The affair cast doubts on his authority at home and his credibility on the international scene. To cut short the delaying tactics of the Gaullist 'rassemblement', the Government turned the Bill authorising the approval of the Brussels agreement into a question of confidence. The Bill was thus passed on 15 June 1977 without a vote. This procedural device, which was hardly satisfactory for the European cause, suited all parties by enabling the Gaullists to avoid a crisis whilst at the same time sparing the Left a public display of disunity. During the parliamentary debate, however, the Government was persuaded to put very precise and restrictive limitations on the powers of the future Assembly. It was forced to go back on the terms of the 1974 Paris communiqué which provided for the extension of the Assembly's powers 'notably by handing over certain powers in the legislative process of the Communities', but, above all, in an unusual step for a ratification authorisation, an additional clause was inserted in the Bill authorising the approval of the international agreement. The text, which was prompted by a Constitutional Council decision of 30 December 1976 recognising the European elections by universal suffrage as constitutional (a victory for President Giscard d'Estaing) but at the same time setting up solid obstacles to prevent national sovereignty being made over to any international organisation (a success for the Gaullists), was the result of long negotiations between the Government and the Gaullist spokesman, Couve de Murville. It amounted to a series of legal guarantees against any extension of the powers of the Assembly of the Communities beyond those strictly laid down in the treaties.

The debate in France was probably not unconnected with the emphasis which the problem of national sovereignty received in Great Britain. The ups and downs of Britain's membership of the Common Market and the important debate which preceded it have been the subject of too many studies for the matter to require further discussion here. In principle, the June 1975 referendum gave final approval to the United Kingdom's membership of the EEC since 67.2 per cent of the voters wanted their country to remain within the Community. And yet the problem of direct elections to the European Parliament, which Harold Wilson had accepted in principle, with some reservations, during the first 'European Council' in Paris in December 1974, gave rise to a new debate which those on the far left of the Labour Party tried to use to revive the issue of Common Market membership. There was at no stage any real possibility of withdrawal, of course, since all parties were obliged to respect the verdict democratically expressed in the June 1975 referendum.

In the first stage, the Green Paper of February 1976, while stressing that Britain accepted the principle of direct elections, emphasised the Community rather than the national aspects of the problem, and forecast, with few regrets, that the difficulties raised as much within the Community as in the other Member States might make it unlikely that the election would be held in 1978. In fact, no serious discussion initiated by the Government took place at Westminster before Spring 1977, even though the agreement on the distribution of seats between the Member States was confirmed in the Brussels Act of 20 September 1976.

At the second stage, after the publication of the April 1977 White Paper[1], when

---

[1] *Direct Elections to the European Assembly,* Cmnd 6768, HMSO, (London, 1977).

it had become necessary to sort out the issue of national sovereignty, the Government, anticipating attacks from part of the Labour Left, announced the introduction of a new clause into the election Bill. This guaranteed that any alteration in the Assembly's powers would require legislation in the British Parliament, and could not simply be introduced under the European Communities Act of 1972. This step put the Government's promise that the EEC would not develop into a federal system into the Bill in black and white. Clause 6, introduced on 17 February 1978, in fact states: 'No treaty providing for any increase whatsoever in the powers of the [European] Assembly will be ratified by the United Kingdom unless it has been approved by an Act of Parliament'. In constitutional terms this clause represented a major innovation, since the ratification of treaties is normally carried out by an 'Order in Council', without the need for legislation.

The ups and downs experienced by the British Parliament in adopting legislation concerning the European elections were directly related to the battle between pro- and anti-Marketeers in the Labour Party. With a few rare exceptions, this division followed the Left-Right split — moderates-extremists, if one prefers — within the Labour Party. The case of Britain, however, is simply the clearest illustration of the primacy of national concerns which dominated this election in all countries, even those which are the strongest supporters of the European cause.

II A National Election Under a European Pretext

In accordance with the 'Act providing for the direct election of representatives to the Assembly of the European Communities by universal suffrage', France, the United Kingdom, Italy and West Germany were each required to nominate 81 representatives under the quota allocated to the four 'major' countries of the Community. In the absence of agreement on a uniform EEC electoral procedure, this Community directive laid down that the election should take place according to each Member State's own procedures. The drawing up of the electoral legislation thus gave rise to difficult discussions throughout the Community.

The electoral legislation
In France, Germany and Italy, the discussions centred on the adoption of a single electoral college or the creation of *ad hoc* constituencies.

In the United Kingdom, in the absence of any debate on ratification itself, it is difficult to unravel the European motivations from those which derived from domestic or party political considerations, in the fight in which the supporters and opponents of proportional representation became involved. Although the Commons Select Committee on direct elections published successive versions of its report in July, August and November 1976, the Government's views were not made public until the appearance of the White Paper of April 1977. And even this did not really commit Mr Callaghan, since he indicated four possible choices of electoral procedure[1] (thus earning for the White Paper the title 'Green and White'), and the discussion on it was not concluded by a vote. At this stage, in fact, the Prime Minister was obliged to take into account two fundamental facts whose consequences were diametrically opposed: on the one hand, the Labour movement's hostility to the European elections and, on the other, the need to ensure the support of the Liberals, since from March 1977 onwards he no longer had a large enough majority in the House of Commons.

---

[1]Under the proposed system of proportional representation, each elector would have a single vote which he could cast in favour of a candidate specially chosen for his region. The votes gained by each party or political grouping in each region would be added together and the seats (about 8 or 9 for each region) would be distributed in proportion to the votes won by each party in the particular region. When a seat became vacant, it would go to the next candidate (by number of votes cast) on that party's list.

Within the Labour Party, hostility to the European elections was further increased after September 1976 when the Party Conference clearly rejected the principle of direct elections by 4,016,000 votes to 1,752,000, thus following a recommendation of the party's Executive Committee. At the parliamentary level, the Tribune group, to which about 80 Members of Parliament from the left wing of the Labour Party belong, actively re-started its anti-European campaign, and the Cabinet itself included several notorious opponents of the European elections. And yet the commitments which had been made to Britain's European partners gave Mr Callaghan very little room for further shilly-shallying. Above all, he had to honour the pact made with the Liberals. This in effect laid down not only that an election should be held (it had in any case been announced in the Queen's Speech), but also that the Government should call for an election by proportional representation. Thus the European Assembly Election Bill was published on 24 June 1977. Although the Government did in fact recommend an election with regional lists and proportional representation, it also made it clear that Parliament, if it so wished, could retain the traditional form of election. But, above all, it was approval of the principle of the European elections which was at issue in this first vote. Approval was obtained on 7 July by a majority of 247 votes, but only thanks to the support of two-thirds of the Conservatives and all of the Liberals, as 132 Labour members voted 'for', 126 voted 'against' (including 26 Ministers and 6 members of the Cabinet), and a further 51 abstained. Although it was part of the Government's programme, Mr Callaghan – in an unprecedented step – did not impose voting discipline and, because of the extreme tension which existed on the European issue, allowed Labour members a free vote in order to avoid a split in the party.

However, as the Bill did not complete all its procedural stages before the end of the parliamentary session, a second Bill was introduced in the autumn, at a time when the Labour Party Conference was again reviving anti-European passions. To short-circuit the Executive Committee's initiatives – it had submitted to Conference a document more or less categorically questioning membership of the EEC – Mr Callaghan had to recommend a kind of European 'Charter' to his party. Whilst excluding the possibility of withdrawal from the Community, he took up certain of the Executive's demands concerning the reform of Community policies, and made no mention at all of the European elections. Somewhat surprised, Conference simultaneously approved both the Executive's document and the Prime Minister's proposals, leaving an ambiguous situation for the future. Moreover, at Westminster, Callaghan decided to push the anti-Europeans within the party further into their entrenched positions. On this occasion a two-line whip, permitting abstention only in the case of long-standing and declared hostility to the European elections, replaced the free vote, and on 24 November the Bill was passed with a majority of 283 votes, as against 247 in the previous vote. Most of the Ministers abstained, amongst them those members of the Cabinet who had voted against the Government in July; 105 other Labour members followed their example, whilst 72 voted against the Bill, together with about 20 Conservatives who on this occasion braved the three-line whip called by their leader. The choice of the electoral system, on which the parties decided to allow a free vote, took place on 13 December. Its concern to maintain the pact with the Liberals, which was dependent if not on the selection of proportional representation then at least on a large number of Labour votes in its favour, led the Government to recommend this system. Added to this was its concern to comply with the Spring 1978 timing laid down by the Nine, which made the drawing up of 81 Euro-constituencies impossible. However, the Prime Minister made it known during the debate that the postponement of the European election 'would not be the end of the world'.

This lukewarm Government support for proportional representation was matched, on the other hand, by the declared opposition of two-thirds of the Conservative Party. Mr Heath and those who supported him on this point were very isolated within a party which, like its new leader Mrs Thatcher, feared that a proportional representation precedent might put an end to the traditional two-party system, and that the Liberals would become the arbitrators of the British political situation. The Conservative vote ensured the defeat of the proposal for proportional representation. This system, which was accepted by all the Liberals and by a majority of the Labour members (147 for, 115 against), was rejected by 196 Conservatives to 61. Thus this parliamentary battle not only revealed, and formed the pretext for, divisions within the Labour Party, forcing Mr Callaghan into performing a dangerous balancing act, but also made clear the nature and the extent of the Conservatives' commitment to Europe.

Although the Conservative Party did not demand a high price for its support for the Labour Government in the successive votes on the issue of direct European elections — without this the Government would have been unable to get the legislation passed — it nevertheless ensured that its domestic political calculations would prevail over European considerations. No doubt the work of the Oxford political scientists had some influence here: according to their estimates for the European election, using the traditional system, a 5 per cent swing to the Conservatives from the 1974 election results would give them 50 seats to Labour's 27, and a 10 per cent swing 61 to 16. On the other hand, the same swing with a system of proportional representation would be less dramatic: 33 seats to 29 or 40 to 23 (in fact, the average voting swing in by-elections between October 1974 and July 1977 was 15 per cent to the Conservatives). The legislation on Europe was finally passed on 16 February 1978 with a majority of 114 votes.

As the traditional voting system was maintained (single member, first past the post), the demarcation of the 81 constituencies, made public at the end of November 1978, presented no major difficulties. Although Scotland, with 8 seats, and Wales with 4, were slighly over-represented in relation to England, with 66, the nationalist parties emphasised their unfair treatment in relation to the small countries in the Community (Denmark, for example, with the same population as Scotland, was to have twice as many Euro-MPs). The Special Commission, which was established to draw up the boundaries, observed two basic principles: keeping the existing parliamentary constituencies undivided, and retaining the unity of the major regions which make up the United Kingdom. The result was Euro-constituencies comprising between 7 and 9 parliamentary constituencies, each with an average electorate of 516,000, although the Scottish Highlands and Islands had only 280,000 while, on the other hand, others, like Glasgow or Kent West, had more than 550,000. For its part, Northern Ireland was to form a single constituency and send three representatives to the European Parliament, elected by the single transferable vote system of proportional representation. This system, which was already in use for local elections, would avoid the risk of an exclusively Protestant contingent of Euro-MPs being elected.

In France, the same concern to make the elections 'as national as possible' dictated the choice of electoral system. The matter was under discussion throughout the whole of 1977. Once agreement had been reached on the choice of proportional representation, there remained the further choice between a single national electoral college or the creation of *ad hoc* constituencies. The Centrists favoured a regionally based election, but neither the Gaullists (who complained of 'this new threat to national unity') nor President Giscard d'Estaing were willing to grant the regions this kind of political force:

> The French Government wishes no more to see Breton, Corsican and Occitan deputies than it desires to have Flemish, Welsh, Bavarian or Sicilian representatives sitting in the European Parliament.[2]

For a while the Elysée favoured a 'multi-departmental' electoral system, but drawing up new constituencies would have aroused countless suspicions and objections, and discredited the whole operation. The selection of a system of proportional representation within a national framework, following the rule of the highest average, with no vote-splitting or preferential votes, appeared to satisfy both the need to respect the unity of the Republic demanded by the Gaullists, and the conditions which the Left had laid down for accepting any proposal concerning the European elections.

To emphasise the 'national' character of the elections, the French Parliament added an amendment to the main body of the Bill, which was more restrictive than the existing rules for French elections, limiting propaganda to 'political parties and lists fighting the election'. The purpose of this was to prevent any involvement in the election campaign by foreign individuals, institutions or political parties. The electoral law was passed with a massive majority: 474 votes to 2 in the National Assembly on 21 June 1977; 256 votes in favour and 20 abstentions in the Senate on 29 June. It set up a double legal and financial barrier: lists which failed to obtain at least 5 per cent of the votes cast would be excluded from the distribution of seats, and would not be able to recover either the compulsory deposit (100,000 francs) or their propaganda expenses (posters, pamphlets). Unlike Italy, France thus adopted a provision which was already in force at the federal level in Germany. President Giscard justified this move on the grounds of his concern 'not to send a divided contingent of representatives to confront the 60 British Conservatives and Germany's 43 Christian Democrats and 34 Socialists'.

In West Germany, the constitutional clause which provides that only those lists which obtain 5 per cent of the votes are eligible for the distribution of seats stems from the idea that small political groups are a danger to the stability of democracy. The small parties asked the Federal Constitutional Court to suspend this clause for

---

[2]Christian Bonnet, Minister of the Interior, to the National Assembly during its first debate on 21 June 1977.

the European election, claiming that it contravened the principle of equality between the parties, that the representation of a variety of political forces would not upset the smooth running of the European Assembly, and that not all of the member countries of the EEC had adopted such restrictive clauses. The Karlsruhe Court rejected this request in the name of parliamentary effectiveness. It claimed that the European Assembly needed to be in a position to exercise its powers when up against the other Community institutions, and that too great a division of its political forces would work against this. It added another powerful argument as a reason for its refusal: small political parties represented by just a few members would not be able to participate in all the Assembly's activities. It was also important that close co-operation should be established between members of the European Parliament and their colleagues in the national Parliaments: small parties which had no members in the Bundestag would be completely cut off from the large representative political forces of West Germany.

This ruling was not adopted elsewhere in the Community. Dealing with a similar request following the election on 10 June 1979, the French Conseil d'Etat refused to make a ruling (decision of 22 October 1979):

> since the rules under attack are concerned with putting the electoral system into practice, with the system of deposits, with the reimbursement by the State of the costs of paper, the printing of voting papers, posters, circulars and advertising expenses, and with the use of the national radio and television networks during the election campaign,

and as these rules were laid down by the law of 7 July 1977,

> it is not for the Conseil d'Etat to take cognizance of any dispute questioning the validity of the provisions of the law.

In West Germany, too, the drafting of the electoral law gave rise to inter-party difficulties. First introduced in the Bundestag (SPD-FDP majority), it was rejected by the Bundesrat (CDU-CSU majority) on 6 May 1977. It was finally passed on 16 March 1978.

In fact, it was not possible to adopt the electoral system which had been in force since 1949, and no single solution was acceptable to all the parties. The mixed electoral system used in the federal elections is based on both a majority vote and a proportional vote. There could be no thought of using this system for the European election, as it would have been necessary to draw up constituencies of more than one million electors, which would have extended over the boundaries of certain small Länder (in 1976 the Saar had 753,786 electors, and Bremen 475,582). These variations had less effect on the nature of the electoral system (proportional representation) than on its administration. The parties in the Government coalition (SPD-FDP) and the Federal Government argued in favour of federal lists of candidates. The Free Democrats feared regional lists restricted to each Land. The differences between the Christian Democratic Union and the Christian Social Union were too great for them to reach agreement on a joint federal list. A system of two separate federal lists, one CDU, the other CSU, would have institutionalised the already fierce competition between the two parties: standing for the first time in an election outside Bavaria, the CSU would have been tempted afterwards to establish a new federal party (a fourth party) which the CDU would not like at all. If they promoted two competing lists, this would, in legal terms, have put an end to the joint CDU-CSU parliamentary group in the Bundestag, in accordance with the rules on parliamentary alliances. At the same time the CDU-CSU would have lost the Presidency of the Bundestag, which would have passed to the SPD. The small liberal party, FDP, which was permanently under threat from the 5 per cent exclusion clause, feared that if the CSU stood throughout the whole country the consequences might be fatal for it. Thus the Government's proposal for federal lists was rejected in the Bundesrat by the CDU-CSU majority, who maintained that this system was unsuitable for West Germany's federal structure: the Christian Democrats gave their support to the regional lists. In the end a compromise was worked out: the voting would be by proportional representation, but each party would have the choice of presenting either a federal list or a Land list (and would be allowed to amalgamate two or more lists).

Unlike the system in the federal and regional elections, the elector would have only one vote. The lists precluded vote splitting or preferential votes. Like most of the Member States of the EEC, West Germany chose to use proportional representation, but it was the only country to use two variants of the system, which inevitably posed certain problems of a legal and political nature.

The three representatives for West Berlin were chosen according to a different system from the one operating in the rest of Germany. When the Act providing for the election of the European Parliament was signed, the Bonn Government made the following statement:

> The Government of the Federal Republic of Germany declares that the Act providing for the election by direct universal suffrage of members of the European Parliament will also apply to the Land of Berlin. In consideration of the rights and responsibilities of France, the United Kingdom of Great Britain and Northern Ireland, and the United States of America, the Berlin Chamber of Deputies will elect the representatives for the seats allocated to the Land of Berlin from among the quota allocated to the Federal Republic of Germany.

Inevitably, the Soviet Government protested vigorously against what it saw as a violation of the Quadripartite Agreement of 3 September 1971. In their reply on 20 September 1976, the Western powers pointed out that the treaties of Rome had already laid down the principle of the direct election of the European Assembly, and that the problem of West Germany's membership of the European Communities had been settled in these treaties. The Western powers did not feel that their rights and responsibilities concerning Berlin had been challenged by the German statement.

In Italy, the choice of an electoral system presented no difficulties. The existing system of proportional representation with a preferential vote possibility, used in the national elections, was retained for the European election with a few slight alterations: in the latter, preferences were not to exceed three (as opposed to four in the legislative elections), and the distribution of seats was to be made using the pure system of proportional representation, and not the adjusted quota system. On the other hand, the time which elapsed between the ratification of the Act and the passage of the election legislation (24 January 1979) is evidence of the problems encountered in drawing up the constituencies. With some difficulty, a compromise was reached between the Government's proposal for the establishment of nine constituencies, and the desire of the smaller parties to have a single national electoral college, which would be more favourable to their representation. The electoral law provided for the division of Italy into five electoral districts. The first district, 'North-West Italy', included Piedmont, the Val d'Aosta, Liguria and Lombardy, and was entitled to 22 seats. The second, 'North-East Italy', included Venetia, Trentino-Alto Adige, Friuli-Venetia Giulia and Emilia-Romagna; the maximum number of representatives was 15. The third, 'Central Italy', brought together Tuscany, Umbria, Marche and Latina, and was allocated 16 seats. The fourth, 'Southern Italy', included the Abruzzi, Molise, Campania, Puglia, Basilicata and Calabria; 19 seats were reserved for this district. The fifth, 'the Italian islands', consisted of Sicily and Sardinia and had an entitlement of 9 seats. Although it was justified by the desire to have better representation of regional interests in Strasbourg, this division caused some confusion, in particular with regard to the inclusion of regions as politically and culturally diverse as 'white' Venetia and 'red' Emilia-Romagna in one single unit.

It should be noted, moreover, that two countries, Italy and West Germany, attempted to give the election a more European flavour by introducing specific arrangements. The law of 24 January enabled Italians living in other member countries of the Community, for the purpose of work or study, to vote in the country where they were living. This measure, intended as an encouragement to an electorate which was expected to be less highly motivated than during a national election, was also a symbol of future European unity. In fact, the administrative difficulties were such that, of 1,200,000 potential electors living in the rest of the Community, only 463,514 were able to register on the electoral rolls in the consulates, and only 136,695 actually voted. On the other hand, the political parties, and especially the left-wing parties, complained that certain host countries — France and Germany — hindered the distribution of electoral propaganda which was directed at emigrants: the exclusive use of the Italian language, meetings allowed only in halls and a ban on outside gatherings, election manifestos to be posted only 48 hours before the vote and in the immediate vicinity of the voting stations, etc.

There is evidence of similar preoccupations in the German regulations: in fact, for the first time an elector of German nationality had the right to vote if he had been resident in one of the other member countries of the EEC for at least three months before the day of the election. This provision represented a change in the electoral law. It affected some 235,000 Germans, of whom about 70 per cent were of voting age.

Drawing up the lists and selecting the candidates
The drawing up of the lists and the selection of the candidates for the European election were done in much the same way as in the national elections. The party leadership exercised more control than usual, except in the case of the British Labour Party where the tradition of giving free rein to the local party committees was maintained. In fact, for the Labour Party, the real business of selection took

11

place at local level, although an outline list was drawn up at Transport House. The task of selection was given to a body consisting of delegates from the parliamentary constituencies within the particular Euro-constituency (25 per constituency). Following an assessment of and interview with the candidates, who were also proposed by the local Labour Party committees (about two or three for each parliamentary constituency), votes were taken until an absolute majority emerged. For the Conservatives, the selection procedure for the Euro-candidates was marked by even greater control than usual by the Central Office in London. 1,050 candidates were put forward, 900 examined and 200 retained. As early as October 1978, a pamphlet about the European elections and in particular the directives relating to the selection of candidates was published, and distributed to the Euro-constituency councils which were specially set up. The national leadership's control was thus clearly visible. Indeed, although the final selection of candidates took place at Euro-constituency level, after the examination of the candidates, interviews, etc., the options were conspicuously limited by the fact that all candidates needed to have a kind of pre-nomination by appearing in the list drawn up in London by a pre-selection committee, the Standing Advisory Committee on European Candidates. At local level, the selection procedure passed through four phases: an examination by a selection committee of the list of candidates standing for nomination in the Euro-constituency; interviews with the candidates, followed by narrowing the list to five candidates, then to two, after the examination by the Euro-constituency council. Finally, the last stage in the selection was carried out by the general assembly of the Euro-constituency, in which at least 25 representatives from each of the parliamentary constituencies within the Euro-constituency took part.

It should be noted that this process involved some serious problems for the candidates who, being able to stand for nomination in some 15 Euro-constituencies, found themselves obliged to travel the whole country to attend their interviews. It also provided some unpleasant surprises for the selection committees, which sometimes found that their preferred candidate had been chosen at the last moment by a faster-working Euro-constituency. On some occasions the local organisations staged a revolt against the central headquarters, and some particularly highly-regarded candidates did not succeed in being selected. This was the case, for example, with the Conservative MP, Paul Channon, who, it was rumoured, might have expected to lead the group in Strasbourg.

The Liberals, for their part, after overcoming their disappointment about the electoral system which penalised them heavily, decided on a selection procedure similar to the one used for national elections, with certain variations from one district to another. No real structure was set up at the Euro-constituency level. In choosing between the candidates who were presented, either individually or by the local party organisations, a combination of two methods was used: voting by the delegates at several points in the constituency, and postal voting by party members.

In Scotland, the Nationalist Party, which has a policy of contesting all elections, had decided to present candidates in the European elections, during its annual conference in 1978. After nomination by the grass roots of the party (at branch level), the candidates were examined by the party's executive committee and a 'national' list was then drawn up and recommended to the selection committees of each Euro-constituency. Nineteen candidates stood for the seven nominations, with one member of the former European Assembly, Mrs Winifred Ewing, being unopposed in the Highlands and Islands constituency.

In France, Italy, and West Germany, the adoption of proportional representation enhanced the centralised nature of the selection procedure. This electoral system calls for the maximum representation of regions and socio-economic groups in the list. In addition, account has to be taken of the different opinions, inclinations and feelings within each of the parties. In each of these countries, the candidate elected by 'the people' was elected in the first instance by the party machinery.

Although the two parties of the Left in France formed their lists as parties, this was not the practice of either the Rassemblement pour la Republique (RPR) or, above all, the Union Démocratique Française (UDF). The list presented by the Communist Party (PCF) was drawn up by the Central Committee after 'consultations with decision-making bodies within the party'. As for the Socialists, 423 members of the PS (including 99 women) presented themselves for selection as candidates. There were consultations in the branches and proposals by the federal commissions, but the 'Socialist list, in association with the left-wing Radicals (MRG)', was drawn up by the Executive Bureau of the Socialist Party after difficult negotiations with the Mouvement des radicaux de gauche (the agreement was signed on 26 April).

On 10 February, in Paris, the Central Committee of the RPR gave 'full powers' to Jacques Chirac to lead and form the list for the 'Defence of France's interests in Europe' (DIFE). It was decided then that the list would have its own organisation, headquarters and general secretary. Chirac was all-powerful at the head of the 'Association for the defence of France's interests in Europe' and, in consultation with Michel Debré, and with the assistance of his principal adviser on the elections, selected the candidates for the DIFE list.

It was no secret that the choice of Simone Veil as head of the Union for France in Europe (UFE) list was made by the Elysée. Moreover, the very loose structure of the UDF, which is not a party but a federation of four parties, clubs, and alliances, meant that top-level arbitration was needed for some serious disagreements between members of the Union and for several specific problems (the candidacy of Jean-Jacques Servan-Schreiber, for example): the arbitrators were Madame Veil and, through her, the Prime Minister and President Giscard d'Estaing.

In Italy, although the regional divisions favoured the selection of local figures with strong personal followings, the role of local and regional federations was considerably weakened by the inclusion in the Euro-constituenceies of several different regions. The regional committees, and in certain cases (especially among the Christian Democrats (DC)) the inter-regional commissions which were set up to examine the candidates, played an entirely marginal role. The decisions were taken at the level of the party leaderships and secretariats, some of whose members, like R. Gaspari, one of the vice-secretaries of the DC, were given the task of dealing with the issue on a 'full-time' basis.

In Germany, the existence of two kinds of list created a quite special situation. The rules of the parties offering federal lists had to be amended to permit the election of delegate assemblies of party members, whose task was to elect candidates for the European elections by secret ballot, and their deputies, previously selected by the proper organs of the party. This system has, at least in theory, the disadvantage of increasing the distance between the candidate and the party member: it reduces the role of local and regional bodies to the benefit of the federal organisations. The Social Democrats (SPD) immediately attempted to reduce these disadvantages by paying special attention to problems of regional balance and, where possible, giving their campaign a regional flavour. Of course, the leaders placed at the head of the lists were well-known, but this was much less true of those lower down the lists, who were perhaps quite unknown outside their own regions. As the voting papers gave only the top ten names on the list, one is bound to wonder whether the elector was not being asked to cast his vote for an anonymous candidate. The system of federal lists also provided certain advantages. Before the meeting of the electoral congress, the party leadership had to agree on the best possible composition of their list and look for a balance between the different interests (political, regional, socio-economic). The counting of votes is also simpler than with regional lists.

The regional lists gave the members and regional organisations of the party a more important role: there is more direct contact between the elector and the elected member, and the particular problems of a region can be dealt with more satisfactorily. But the disadvantages are not inconsiderable: the diversity of the lists is not consistent with a balanced parliamentary representation between the different Länder, and vote-counting is also more complicated. This is especially true as the lists can be regrouped to include several Länder. This procedure was adopted to enable the small Länder (Bremen and Saar) to have a representative in Europe by establishing one large Land. The distribution of seats is allocated by the highest average according to the d'Hondt system. If a candidate presents himself in two Länder and is elected on both lists, he takes his mandate from the list in which he is best placed. The dual lists present the problem of candidates' equality before the election. It is more difficult to gain a nomination as a candidate at the federal than at the regional level. The relationship between the elected representative and the elector is different, according to whether the representative presents himself on a federal or on a regional list.

Is there a profile of the 'typical Euro-candidate'?
What criteria were used in the different countries in selecting the candidates? Here again, national considerations have made it impossible to characterise a typical Euro-candidate. Although in Italy and West Germany the candidates showed positive feelings towards Europe, indeed almost a militant commitment, this was not the case in France and Britain, where strikingly different attitudes towards Europe could be found between one political group and another, and sometimes within the same party. But in no case was the candidate's attitude towards Europe the most important issue. When the lists were being compiled, the concern to represent differing views within the parties, well-known personalities, people from the party organisation, regional interests, and socio-economic groups, and to leave room for women, produced some subtle calculations.

But, here again, in some respects the United Kingdom is a special case. For the British Liberals, a commitment to Europe goes without saying, but it was also an essential condition of nomination for the Conservatives, where the minority in the party which still remains distrustful of the EEC was ruthlessly set aside when the national list was being compiled. The Labour left-wing, for its part, tried to ensure ideological unity among the Labour candidates by endeavouring to keep out the pro-Europeans. For example, on the initiative of certain members of the Executive Committee close to Tony Benn, a questionnaire enabling candidates too much in favour of the Community to be identified was sent to members of the Labour selection committees. Of course, the Labour Committee for Europe replied by suggesting to the candidates suitable replies to these embarrassing questions but, with the predominance of anti-Marketeers within the party organisation, one might have feared that an overwhelming majority of candidates opposed to Europe would be chosen by the local selection committees. In fact, it seems that about one third of the candidates were committed anti-Europeans, one third were well-known Europeans, and a final third claimed to want to reform the Community rather than to withdraw from it.

Of course, in many cases candidates were able to overcome the handicap of their commitment to Europe by their experience in local affairs. Labour in fact put up almost three times as many candidates with links in local politics as their Conservative opponents (41 as against 15). Inasmuch as it had rejected the dual mandate, the Labour Party offered hardly any candidates with experience of national politics, with the exception of two retiring MPs (including the former Cabinet Minister, Barbara Castle) who were thus withdrawing from Westminster, one former member of the House of Commons, and twenty or so former parliamentary candidates. In addition, by choosing not to select a single member of the House of Lords, the Labour Party took no advantage of the fact that on this occasion members of the Upper House were eligible for election (the former Labour Foreign Secretary, Lord George Brown was nominated as an 'Independent' though he withdrew before polling day). There were a large number (29) of university and polytechnic lecturers and a mere 4 businessmen amongst the Labour candidates (the figures were exactly the reverse for the Conservatives). On the other hand, the list included very few manual workers (4) and trade unionists (6), no doubt because the system of trade union sponsorship of candidates was not used in the European election. Labour put up fewer women candidates (8) than the Conservatives (10) but they got relatively better treatment from Labour, as their constituencies were safer (4 women for 18 seats considered to be safe).

The Conservative candidates compensated for their lesser experience in local affairs with greater political experience, since their numbers included five retiring MPs, one former MP, six peers, and numerous former parliamentary candidates. But perhaps European experience was a more important criterion for selection than parliamentary experience. Diplomats, European officials and journalists appeared high on the list alongside those professions which are supposed to promote rapid European 'socialisation': bankers, businessmen, etc. In a study published by the weekly *New Society*, David Butler and his colleagues identified 31 Conservatives with European ties as opposed to 3 Labour candidates, with genuine 'Eurocrats' numbering 10 amongst the Conservatives and only one of the Labour candidates.[3] Although there were no manual workers or trade unionists on the Tory list, there were seven farmers (including the former President of the National Farmers' Union, Sir Henry Plumb) as against none at all on the Labour list. Finally, 10 women were selected, of whom in the event 6 were elected.

Although the electoral system inevitably tended to turn the election into a duel between Labour and the Conservatives, it is interesting to look at the position of the other parties' candidates. The Liberals appealed mainly to the candidates whom they normally put up at parliamentary elections, with these accounting for 60 of the 81 on the list. There were also one member of the House of Commons, three peers and three 'Eurocrats'. The professions, including university teaching, were particularly well represented, and five women were nominated.

The Scottish National Party chose its candidates from amongst the party's well-known figures, notably its president, R. MacIntyre, and Mrs Winifred Ewing, who was a member of the previous European Assembly, but who had been defeated in the parliamentary election of 3 May.

In France there was sometimes a conflict between the concern to represent all shades of opinion and the wish to offer a coherent programme. Of the four main lists, those chosen by the Communists and the Gaullists were the only ones which escaped this dilemma. In the PCF 'democratic centralism' operated perfectly: there were no 'challengers' among the candidates. Of the twenty most highly placed candidates, ten were members of the Political Bureau or of the Central Committee. The list was headed by the party's General Secretary. The candidates committed themselves 'resolutely to defend France's independence and the sovereignty of her people, and to safeguard their interests'. The list was 'open' to only three individuals who were not members of the PCF: the General Secretary of the Communist Party of the island of Réunion, the General Secretary of the Union Progressiste (Progressive Union – the PCF's 'fellow-traveller'), and the General Secretary of the Fédération nationale des producteurs de vin de table (the National Wine-producers' Federation), all three of whom were placed in a good position on the list to be elected.

There was relative homogeneity too in the DIFE list. 'European' Gaullists were excluded from it as were the 'opposition' Gaullists. All the candidates agreed to a 'Charter of the 81' which was based on two guiding principles: 'a European Organisation is essential' and 'the Europe of the future will not be built on the ruins of states and the weakening of nations'. The list wanted to see itself as 'united' around one stipulation: fidelity to the memory of General de Gaulle and to Gaullism, as it is conceived by Jacques Chirac.

Conversely, the composition of the list of the Socialist Party (PS) and the Radicaux de Gauche (MRG) rested largely on the balance between the various factions within the PS which had emerged from the congress in Metz in April (Mitterrand 40.11 per cent; Mauroy 13.61 per cent; Rocard 20.41 per cent;

---

[3]David Butler *et al.* 'The Euro-persons', *New Society*, 3 May 1979. The above details are also based on the parties' own publications about their candidates.

CERES[4] 14.43 per cent). The need to combine a balance between these 'factions' with a 'regional' balance caused Edgard Pisani to be shifted from fourteenth to twenty-third place, which ran the risk of depriving the PS and France of one of its most influential spokesmen in Strasbourg. The first of the MRG's candidates came only sixth on the list, after a representative of each of the main factions. The agreement between the PS and the MRG providing for eight MRG candidates to be included in the list, only two of whom would be in a position to secure election — Maurice Faure, sixth place and R.G. Schwartzenburg, twentieth place — was mainly a result of Mitterand's personal wishes, and provoked serious controversy even within the PS. The list was drawn up in consideration of internal party politics almost to the exclusion of all else. The list of highest-placed candidates included a number from the party machine in Paris, several of whom had 'failed the test of universal suffrage'. It is clear that the inclusion on the same list of candidates from different factions whose views on Europe varied considerably damaged the coherence of the PS's campaign, and reinforced the 'personalisation' around Mitterrand, who headed the list.

However, the most difficult political 'patchwork' to achieve was the list led by Simone Veil. This list had a clearly 'Government' appearance: it was officially supported by the Prime Minister and included four Ministers in office, one of whom headed the list, and two of whom were in positions where they could expect to be elected. The list was united around 'support for the European policy of the President of the Republic'. On the other hand, the need to represent the diverse groups within the UDF (Parti républicain, Social-Democratic Centre (CDS), Parti radical, clubs Perspectives et Réalités, Mouvement des démocrates socialistes français) led to the inclusion of a number of candidates who were known in the past for their views in favour of a supra-national Europe and for their opposition to General de Gaulle's European policy (Jean Lecanuet and Pierre Pflimlin) in a list whose official propaganda constantly maintained that its programme and aims were directly in line with those of the General and of George Pompidou! Finally, the list's political range, in which all the opinions and political preferences within the governing coalition's electorate could be found, was completed by a number of well-known personalities.[5] The opposing parties, notably the supporters of the DIFE list, made much play of denouncing the 'confusion' and 'incoherence' of the Veil list whose members came from different schools of thought and who, after election, would sit some with the Christian Democrats and others with the Liberals.

In varying degrees each of the four major political groups took account of the expertise in European affairs of the individuals appearing on their lists, but none of them took this as the most important criterion. The attempt to achieve a regional balance was particularly emphasised by the parties of the Left who presented their

---

[4]Centre d'Etudes de Recherche et d'Education Socialiste.

[5]Edgar Faure, an RPR deputy, appeared in third place on the UDF list as a member of the Radical party, but without the consent of the party's leadership. A former MRG official, Henri Caillavet, stood as 'an elected member of the opposition'. The 81st place was occupied by a Compagnon de la Libération, Eugène Claudius-Petit.

candidates on a regional rather than departmental basis. These parties also attached more importance to the representation of women than did the parties on the government side. In addition, all the groups were careful to include representatives of the overseas departments in their lists.

Although the Communist Party succeeded in keeping a balance between manual workers and intellectuals, and between urban and rural areas, the Socialist Party, in trying continually to maintain a balanced representation of opinion within the party, experienced much more difficulty in reconciling a suitable socio-economic distribution with a fair representation of the different factions.

In trying to win the support of the same electorate, the two groups on the government side shared the same concerns: to have prominent individuals with influence in local affairs, and representing the largest possible number of socio-economic groups.

One of the most prominent 'pro-European' personalities in France appeared at the head of the DIFE list. A strange paradox! But one which Louise Weiss, one of the leading figures on the list, resolved quite simply when, contradicting Jacques Chirac's and Michel Debré's entire campaign, she stated: 'The views which are held by the President of the Republic and by M. Chirac on Europe are not so different as people are saying' (*Le Monde*, 14 April 1979).

Mayors of large towns, representatives of the professions, experts on maritime affairs and Breton fishermen, small and medium-sized companies and the Catholic teaching profession were all simultaneously wooed by the UDF and the RPR. As the weeks passed, they were a source of great amusement to observers, as they used their best techniques of persuasion in the attempt to win support.

All the four political groups directed extra special efforts on the one hand towards the regions which are affected by Community policies (the wine-growing South, the steel-producing areas in the North and in Lorraine), and on the other towards the group which has the most direct interest in the Common Market: the farmers. Each of the lists tried to include among its candidates an important figure from the rural world. The RPR counterbalanced the inclusion of Michel Debatisse (President of the Fédération nationale des syndicats d'exploitants agricoles – the National Farmers' Union) on the Veil list by including Hubert Buchon, another important farming personality. The PS countered the PCF's inclusion of the influential president of the Wine-producers' Federation, Emmanuel Maffre-Baugé, with Georges Sutra (a wine-grower).

Although all the large parties had an abundance both of candidates and of attempts to secure their support (this was especially true of the UDF and the Socialists), the small political groups experienced much difficulty in finding 81 candidates, and the leaders of their lists had to undertake the difficult task of finding volunteers.

In Italy, the greater freedom of the European election in comparison with the national elections (which were dominated by the Christian Democrat-Communist debate) led to an expectation that part of the electorate would use preferential voting to give priority to the quality or prestige of the individual candidates. In this respect, three criteria common to all the political groups influenced the selection of candidates: political importance, personal prestige, and European experience.

All the parties were represented by their national secretaries (Zaccagnini for the Christian Democrats, Berlinguer for the Communists (PCI), Craxi for the Socialists (PSI) and Almirante for the right-wing Movimento Sociale Italiano (MSI)) or by top-level leaders like Mauro Ferri, former General Secretary of the Social-Democrats (PSDI), and Marco Pannella, the real leader of the Radical Party. Men of such political importance as Flaminio Piccoli, president of the Christian Democrats, and Giancarlo Pajetta, member of the PCI leadership responsible for the party's foreign relations, also appeared among the candidates.

Outside the party membership, intellectuals and cultural figures were especially sought after. Indeed, many agreed to appear on a party's list in a position which gave them virtually no chance of being elected in order that their names could be used as a kind of guarantee. With the exception of a few important writers such as Messrs Sciascia, put up by the Radical Party in five constituencies, Sanguinetti, a PCI candidate, and Strehler, standing for the Socialists (all unsuccessfully), the intellectuals were drawn mainly from journalism or the universities. The party which, proportionately, received the support of the largest number of intellectuals was the Radical Party (apart from Sciascia, one can note such names as Macciocchi, Melega, and Alberti, among others). The party with least support from this quarter was the neo-fascist party, the MSI.

Finally, the third criterion, and no doubt the most important, was the European experience of the majority of the candidates. Apart from the big names of European politics such as Emilio Colombo, president of the former Assembly, Mario Rumor and Giorgio Amendola, former presidents respectively of the Christian Democrat and Communist Parliamentary groups in Strasbourg, Altiero Spinelli (independent on the Communist list), a former Commissioner in Brussels, or Fabrizia Baduel Glorioso, president of the Community's Economic and Social Committee, there were also a fair number of candidates who had already represented their parties in Strasbourg. Because of the regional divisions, all the political parties called on personalities who had a considerable local following. One could mention Sergio Pininfarina (PLI), president of the Turin industrial union, in the first electoral district, Carlo Ripa di Meana (PSI), former president of the Venice Biennale, in the second electoral district, Pancrazio De Pasquale (PCI), president of the Sicilian region, and Salvatore Lima (DC), former mayor of Palermo, in the fifth electoral district.

As for the representation of socio-economic groups, a special place was reserved for trade unionists and for top businessmen. Thus Luigi Macario gave up his position as general secretary of the Confederazione Italiana Sindicati dei Lavoratori (CISL) in order to stand as a Christian Democrat in the European election, and the Socialist Party gave a top place to Mario Dido, one of the national secretaries of the Confederazione Generale Italiana del Lavoro (CGIL), while Aldo Bonaccina, another secretary of the CGIL, stood for the Communists (all three are or have been members of the EEC's Economic and Social Committee). As for the industrialists, this time, rather than delegate the protection of their interests and values to the professional politicians, top businessmen were more directly involved in the campaign. Mostly, their names appeared in the lists of the Liberal or Republican parties. They were not completely absent from the lists of the Christian Democrats, but here they were generally representatives of small or medium-sized companies, or of large farming interests (Alfredo Diana, for example, the former leader of the Confagricultura). One further group was slightly better represented than during national elections: women, who on this occasion were relatively well placed, although they were rarely in a position to be elected. However, three women were at the head of their lists: Leonilde Jotti (PCI) in the second electoral district, Susanna Agnelli (PRI) in the first, and Luciana Castellina (PDUP) in the third.

Finally, certain candidates were an electoral platform in themselves. The most striking example is that of Jeri Pelikan, famous for his role in Czechoslovakia in 1968, whose selection by the Socialist Party is an indication both of the importance the Socialist Party attaches to civil rights and individual liberties, and of its blatantly polemical attitude towards the Communist world. One might also note the large number of 'independent' candidates on the lists of the PCI — generally names well-known in Europe like Altiero Spinelli or Fabrizia Baduel Glorioso — which reflected both the party's concern to demonstrate its openness to non-marxist schools of thought and its commitment to Europe.

No standard profile of the German candidates in the European elections can be discerned. At first, the parties were concerned with fairly well agreed criteria: the candidate must be available (thus avoiding dual mandates), and must show some previous experience either in parliamentary or in European affairs (knowledge of at least one language from another country in the Community was also required). The number of citizens who felt they conformed to this description was so large that the party leaderships were literally inundated with offers of candidates and letters of recommendation. The result of this onslaught was the much greater involvement of regional and federal organisations in the selection of candidates than is usually the case in the federal elections. Very soon, the careful arrangements made by the parties, which had promised to provide a rigorous selection procedure, fell to pieces because of the numerous and contradictory issues at stake. As in the other countries, it was important to maintain a careful balance. The attempt to deal with all these issues at the regional level was like trying to achieve the impossible. The lists of deputy candidates gave a certain amount of flexibility. The major parties all nominated a deputy for each candidate, in some cases giving the deputy quite a realistic chance of election. The practice of holding a dual mandate was more widespread than the parties had at first wished, and women were not allowed to fight the large number of seats which they were initially promised. The lists were also characterised by the advanced age of those heading them, by the inclusion of former political leaders whom the parties held in high regard, and by the fact that many candidates were virtually unknown.

The SPD list, led by Willy Brandt, included three trade union leaders amongst its top eight candidates — a fact which gave rise to much discussion about the neutrality of the trade unions. Martin Bangemann, head of the FDP list, sharply attacked the 'trade union state', and was fond of claiming 'We are not building a workers' Europe or an employers' Europe, but a Europe of citizens'. Heinz Oscar Vetter, president of the Trade Union Federation (DGB), in second place on the SPD's list, immediately below Willy Brandt, replied that the European Assembly elections offered a unique opportunity for the workers, which the latter could not afford to let pass, that the DGB remained completely independent of the SPD, but that there was common ground in the two programmes. The employers' and farming organisations gave fairly open support to the CDU-CSU lists. For tactical reasons, the CDU refrained from criticising the DGB directly, unlike the CSU which maintained that, by offering candidates, the trade unions became political opponents, who in future would have to be dealt with as such. In a letter of 22 January 1979, the general secretary of the CSU called upon the DGB's candidates to resign from their trade union offices. The CSU president, Franz-Josef Strauss, immediately accused the trade unions of conspiring to use European co-operation to introduce collectivism and Communism to West Germany. Apart from the trade union leaders, the SPD list included Katharina Focke (former Minister of Health and for Youth, and former director of a European research institute), Heinz Kuhn (former Minister-President of North Rhine-Westphalia), Rudi Arndt (former mayor of Frankfurt), Thomas von der Vring (former President of the University of Bremen), and Heidemarie Wieczorek-Zeul (former President of the Young Socialists).

The FDP list was led by the party's former general secretary, Martin Bangemann. 'Ex' officials dominated the top of the CDU and CSU lists, but two candidates were particularly notable. Hans Jahn, a member of the Bundestag and already a member of the European Assembly, led the CDU list for Lower-Saxony. His candidature would no doubt have passed unremarked had not the weekly magazine *Stern* made certain revelations concerning the violently anti-semitic content of Jahn's writings during the war; in fact, Jahn's commitment to nazism was already well-known, but the showing of the American television series 'Holocaust' made journalists more sensitive to this theme. Despite pressure from within West Germany as well as from abroad, Jahn refused to resign before the elections, but was forced to do so afterwards. Much attention was also drawn to the Bavarian list by the inclusion of Otto von Habsburg, son of the former Emperor of Austria-Hungary, who had acquired German nationality the previous year, and who, in 1961, had officially renounced his claim to his Austrian titles and property. He was well-known for his European militancy, for his numerous publications, and for his activities as leader of the Pan-European Movement; it was also known that he worked for the Seidel Foundation which is closely linked with the CSU. His candidature, put forward by Franz-Josef Strauss, President of the CSU and Minister-President of Bavaria, caused a stir even within the party. Some of its leaders were worried about the queries which might be raised concerning Otto von Habsburg's democratic beliefs. But Strauss placed more confidence in him as a candidate who would attract support from the most conservative sections in the electorate, where monarchism is still a potent force.

The problem of the dual mandate
The holding of a European mandate together with a mandate for a national Parliament is permitted under the election legislation in all four countries. This arrangement has the three-fold aim of ensuring the co-ordination of the European Assembly's activities with national policies, of enabling the party organisations to exercise some control over the representatives in Strasbourg and, less importantly, of preventing the European Assembly from being used as a 'gilded retirement-home' for second-rate politicians. However, the various political parties resolved the

problem of the dual mandate in different ways. Only the Italian Liberals and the British Labour Party, for quite opposite reasons, have banned it completely. Two Labour MPs, for example, who were well-known for their commitment to Europe, Sir Geoffrey de Freitas and Colin Phipps, had to give up their national mandates in order to canvass for European nominations which they finally failed to obtain. Although the Conservatives did not object to the principle, they nevertheless did not accept many dual mandates, fearing, as they approached a General Election, that they might gain only a small majority in the House of Commons. Thus only five Conservative MPs canvassed for seats in Strasbourg. This common attitude towards dual mandates on the part of the two main British parties was no doubt responsible for the fact that, contrary to what was happening in the other countries of the Community, neither of them chose well-known national figures as candidates for the European elections, the single exception being the Labour Party's Barbara Castle, one of the most prominent personalities in British politics, who was not standing for election at Westminster. The Conservatives, who claimed to be the European party, offered no-one with this kind of parliamentary and ministerial experience, no doubt because the most prominent figures in the party were more interested in a position in a future Tory government than in a seat in the European Assembly.

On the other hand, in Italy, the Christian Democrats and the Social Democrats, who had supported a ban on dual mandates, permitted some exceptions to this rule for their important party leaders. In France the RPR expressed its reservations about the dual mandate in yet another way. After declaring its opposition, and even proposing legislation on the matter, it changed its tactics and adopted a rotation system under which each of the 81 candidates on the DIFE list undertook, if elected, to resign at the end of one year so that there would be a turnover of representatives. The most ardent supporters of the dual mandate were probably the French and Italian Communists, who were anxious to ensure that their parties retained control over their Euro-deputies and over the decisions taken in Strasbourg.

Curiously, the holding of the European election and the problem of the dual mandate caused scarcely any progress to be made in the debate about the links which would have to be established between members of the national and of the European Parliaments. Particularly in the two countries where national sovereignty was the major issue, the question was resolved in quite different ways. In France the establishment of 'parliamentary delegations', whose job was to provide reports on the European Assembly's activities to the French Parliament, gave the latter the main responsibility for controlling the Euro-deputies.

In Britain, on the other hand, bearing in mind the rare occurrence of the dual mandate, several proposals were made with a view to preventing the European representatives from losing contact with national politics and from supporting a different line from that being taken at Westminster. At present, although the need for a link between the European representatives and the members of the national Parliament is not disputed, a consensus seems to be emerging on leaving the responsibility in this matter to the political parties. This was, in any case, the opinion of Douglas Hurd, the Conservative spokesman on European affairs, who stated in *The Times* on 25 July 1978,

The European Parliament, like the Westminster Parliament, is organised on party lines, and the main responsibility for the relationship between the two will lie with the political parties. That is not to say that party discipline could be as strict in the European Parliament as it is at Westminster. But it is essential that they and their staffs should be meshed into their political parties at home at all levels.

For its part, the Labour Party Executive tackled the problem of communication and discipline before the election, by requiring its candidates 'to remain loyal to the Manifesto drawn up for the European election, and to comply with directives given by the Labour group in the European Assembly and approved by the National Executive Committee'.

These questions about the nature of the links to be created between the two Parliaments open up a more fundamental issue: should the European representatives be simply an extension of their national Parliaments, or should they become a new kind of 'political animal'? The first election by universal suffrage lends hardly any support to the latter prospect, to the extent that national issues dominated the election and that the European issue was mainly 'instrumentalised' to serve domestic ends.

The domestic stakes

The European election campaign appeared as an extension of the domestic political debate (in either a major or a minor way) in three of the four countries under consideration, and as an opportunity for modifying it in the fourth, Italy.

It was probably in West Germany that narrow national issues were least prominent. However, the national issues which had been the basis of the CDU-CSU's election campaign in 1976 ('freedom or socialism') were used in the European campaign when European issues (the 35-hour week, for example) were adopted by the SPD for domestic party political ends. Some animosity resulted from the fact that the political parties feared, or pretended to fear, that their political opponents would make use of Europe to achieve objectives which had hitherto been unsuccessful. The Christian Democrats accused the SPD of wanting to push West Germany towards socialism, and the Social Democrats feared that the CDU-CSU, strengthened by its support in Europe, might return to power in Bonn and succeed in introducing its conservative policies there.

Finally, a study of the election campaign in Germany shows that the traditional conflicts over domestic political issues arose in just the same way as in a normal legislative election. Before the poll, the European election was often presented as a kind of trial run for the 1980 federal elections, for which it was necessary to make a start a good year beforehand. After the 10 June elections, in which the opposition parties were victorious over the parties of the governing majority, everyone emphasised that the two kinds of election were not comparable.

In Britain, the European election was merely 'a post-script to the general election . . . a minor extension of British political life'. This phrase of the Liberal leader, David Steel, during his press conference on 29 May 1979, neatly sums up a situation for which he blamed the Conservatives and the Labour Party, even though one might object that, despite its undeniable European convictions, his party also made use of the European election to make a domestic point, namely to demonstrate the iniquities of the British electoral system. In Northern Ireland and Scotland, the question of a European election campaign was not even raised. In the one case because Europe is hardly an important issue compared with the problems confronting the province, in the other because the recent failure of devolution made it difficult to 'sell' a Scottish policy for Europe to the electorate, and because the SNP since that time had mainly stressed the opportunity offered in Europe for by-passing the Westminster Parliament. To a great extent, in fact, the battle between the two major parties was a repetition and an extension of the European dimension of the general election, with one party rallying to the EEC because it reflected its ideology and lent it support, the left-wing of the other party criticising it for the opposite reasons.

In addition, although the Labour left-wing saw the fight against the Conservatives and that against the Community as a single and undivided issue, the European election also formed a domestic issue insofar as it constituted one episode amongst others in the left-wing's battle with the moderates and the party leader, James Callaghan. In fact, Tony Benn explicitly linked the European issue with this battle in order to introduce his own ideas on democracy within the Labour Party. 'If a Labour Prime Minister had less patronage and if MPs were subject to re-selection, the country would not be in the EEC now,' he claimed. 'To stand against the Community is to stand for democratic socialism.' Such a position can be better understood if one is aware that Benn, having declined the opportunity to stand as a candidate for the Shadow Cabinet, is campaigning for changes in the procedure for selecting the leader of the Parliamentary Labour Party and the Shadow Cabinet, and for greater grass-roots influence on the policies of the party and on the selection of election candidates. Because he was certain of a sympathetic audience among the grass-roots of the party, which remained very largely anti-European, the argument which he developed concerning Common Market membership thus served as part of a long-term strategy for achieving power within the party.

In France one year after the legislative elections which had accentuated the four-way political divisions of the country, and two years before the major event of the presidential election, domestic issues were in the forefront of the debate. The 1979 results would determine the 1981 strategies. For the immediate future, the leaders of each list, several of whom were risking their own political futures, wanted to reinforce their political groups at home and to strengthen them in relation to other groups in the same political 'camp'. This requirement determined how the lists standing for election made their tactical choices and drew up their programmes, often to the detriment of transnational solidarity.

Although the Giscardians, following the lead of the President of the Republic, had always maintained that the European election campaign was not a domestic political issue, the tasks allocated to the UDF were clear: partly to reduce the strength of the RPR within the majority, by taking enough of its traditional votes to weaken it, and partly to take a slice of the Socialist electorate by challenging the PS for the centrist and pro-European fringe. Faced with the 'Gaullism-crushing machinery' set up by the Giscard administration, the RPR had to show that its voice counted in the majority and would count in Strasbourg. What better ground than foreign policy for reasserting the Rassemblement's identity and demonstrating its distinctiveness? Had not the unity of the Gaullists always centred around national independence and the fight against submission?

Despite these not inconsiderable tactical concerns, the Gaullists' mistrust of the ability — and the will — of the Government and the Head of State to defend national sovereignty within the Community was nevertheless real. The President of the Republic's commitment to Gaullism (restated in Giscard d'Estaing's press conferences on 21 November 1978 and 15 February 1979), and that of his supporters, was received with scepticism. Jacques Chirac spoke of 'a misappropriation of the inheritance' and of 'an abhorrent attempt to regain ground'. Throughout the campaign he denounced the hypocrisy of those 'who, in 1965, claimed with M. Lecanuet the honour of having forced a second round on General de Gaulle' (in the Presidential elections) 'and who, today, are trying to usurp his heritage'. He added 'the Fouchet Plan was sabotaged with the help of the centrists who are now on Madame Veil's list. We cannot accept this deceit.'

On the left, the Socialist Party deliberately chose to centre the debate on the domestic scene. François Mitterrand declared at his press conference on 23 April, when the Socialist campaign was launched:

> How can one expect that the severe judgement which the French people are making on the Giscard-Barre government will not also extend to their views about the future of Europe? Domestic political issues will determine the outcome to the extent that the French people do not wish to entrust their fate in Europe to those who have deceived them in France.

With the presidential elections in prospect, the stakes were important for Mitterrand. The PS had to confirm the progress which had made it 'France's foremost party' and had swung the balance on the Left in its favour: the poll needed also to reinforce the PS's internal 'majority dynamics' and to secure the first secretary's position within his party. The challenge was a subtle one: on the one side the party had to demonstrate that it was pro-European without belonging to Giscard's camp, on the other that it was possible to be an internationalist and still be a good Frenchman. The French Communist Party, for its part, had to cope with none of these contradictions. Internally, the stakes were clear: the PCF, for which an 'historic decline' was forecast, and which was afraid of becoming 'marginal', needed to prove that it could maintain its position at home and that it could not be reduced to an 'additional force' within the French Left. It mobilised its troops in an unambiguous position and attempted to win the votes of all those who opposed the Government's policy. The introduction of proportional representation into the habits of an electorate, which for the last twenty years had been told of the stabilising virtues of the majority system for national elections, gave the election a certain special character. The election, it was said, would show the exact outline of French political representation: it was often said that, coming two years before the presidential elections, the European elections would be a '100 per cent opinion poll'.

The dramatising of the domestic debate in France monopolised the attention of observers, but surely it was in Italy that the stakes, in terms of the political system, were the most important. The Italian tradition of looking to foreign policy for a

25

solution to domestic difficulties was reinforced by the coincidence of the European poll and a legislative election, whose date had been brought forward.

In a highly charged atmosphere, in which all the political strategies — historic compromise, national unity, return to the centre-left — were brought into play, most of the parties saw the election as a way of altering the balance of political forces and, more importantly, of changing the 'abnormal' nature of the Italian political system. Socialists, Social Democrats, Republicans and Liberals all looked to Europe for the same beneficial effects, and above all for a very marked reduction in the importance of the Communist Party. While the PCI had 34.4 per cent of the votes and 227 seats in the National Assembly elected in 1976, just before the elections the EEC experts were predicting that the Communist group at the Assembly in Strasbourg would gain 44 out of 410 seats. They were also hoping that the PCI's shift towards democratic socialism, which implied a progressive renunciation of its ideological positions and its links with the Soviet Union, would be speeded up. Furthermore, they were counting on a progressive disappearance of the understanding between the two 'doctrinal' parties, DC-PCI, which was stifling the intermediate parties.

At the same time, Europe provided an additional opportunity for these parties by offering them strong power-bases. Though weak at the national level (PSI, 9.6 per cent of the votes and 57 seats; PSDI, 3.4 per cent of the votes and 15 seats; PRI, 3.1 per cent of the votes and 14 seats; PLI, 1.3 per cent of the votes and 5 seats), at the European level they could count on a considerably stronger position. In fact, the polls were attributing 110 seats to the Socialist-Social Democrat group to which the PSI and PSDI belonged, and 40 seats to the Liberal-Democrat group to which the PRI and PLI belonged. For the Liberal Party and the Social-Democratic Party, which were handicapped at the national level (the former by a long and well-established decline which had brought it from 7 per cent of the votes in 1963 to 1.3 per cent, that is to the point of virtual disappearance, in 1976; the latter by the politico-financial scandals which had cost its general secretary a prison sentence), Europe was indeed the only possible means of returning to political influence. For its part, the PSI gambled its entire political strategy on the 10 June results. In fact, it was in Europe that it hoped to find the answer to the interminable question which it had been debating since 1946: the relationship between its reformist vocation and its connection with the Communist Party. Its two contrasting experiences, 'frontist' (1946-56) and centre-left (1962-76), had in fact only succeeded in further widening the gulf between a Socialist Party (reduced by 1976 to 9.6 per cent of the votes) and a strong Communist Party (with 34.4 per cent of the votes). Thus its domestic situation seemed almost insoluble, caught, as it was, between an impossible alternative on the Left and a suicidal return to a subordinate position in alliance with the Christian Democrats. On the other hand, the reversal of the balance of forces on the Left in Europe gave it back its freedom of action. In European politics, the Socialists were in a position to deal with the Christian Democrat group on an equal footing and were in an overwhelmingly superior position in relation to the Communist group. This reversal of the Socialists' and Communists' roles also had another advantage. In a European system which emerges as an opposition between two blocs, the one progressive and dominated by the Socialists, the other Conservative and dominated by the Christian Democrats, the Italian DC is no longer that large popular inter-class party, which is the necessary basis of any coalition (centre-right, centre, centre-left or national unity), and becomes the moderate pole of a bipartite system.

Although alternation in power between the conservatives and the progressives is very much in line with the interests of the PSI, it is the exact opposite of the Christian Democrat strategy, which is based on a system in which the centre — which it firmly occupies itself — and not the left or right wing is in control. Thus the DC did not share the hopes of the secular parties for a European solution to Italian problems, except so far as the Communist problem was concerned.

The position of the Communist Party is even more complicated. On the one hand, it is clear that one of the reasons which led it to provoke a governmental crisis in January, thereby ensuring that the date of the national election would be before that of the European poll, was to test its strength in Italy before the general weakness of the Communist movement in Europe became apparent. It was a decision which the Socialists had scarcely any difficulty in representing as a 'decision against Europe'. On the other hand, its European commitment was dictated by the overriding concern of gaining the legitimation at the international level which it had already achieved at home through its participation in the ruling majority in Parliament.

III National Convergences, Transnational Party Dimensions and Cross-cutting Affinities

It would be wrong to limit the lessons to be drawn from the European elections simply to issues of domestic political balance. Over and above the ambiguities and tactical concerns, in each country the campaign brought out, at national level, common concerns and serious questions about the development of the Common Market in certain spheres. By stating common national concerns, the campaign put the transnational links formed by most of the European parties to the test. It gave rise to affinities both between countries and between parties which challenge the existence of political partnerships and transnational 'families' which are all too easily presented as realities.

National convergences

Can one possibly speak of a 'national' attitude towards Europe in connection with Britain, when it is in this country that the very principle of Community membership arouses the most passionate divisions?

If the problem of membership affects only a minority inside the Conservative Party, which is on the whole committed to European unity, the publications and the campaign of the Labour Party could lead one to believe that belonging to the EEC is not an irreversible matter. For example, in Labour's manifesto, one finds the following assertion, by way of conclusion:

> We declare that if the fundamental reforms contained in this manifesto are not achieved within a reasonable period of time, then the Labour Party would have to consider very seriously whether continued EEC membership was in the best interests of the British people.

Now the conditions which it lays down clearly amount to the destruction of the present Community. In the legal sphere, for example, the requirements concerning national sovereignty, as it is conceived in this document, would involve removing the direct applicability of some of the Community legislation and according Westminster the right to reject, change or repeal it. This clearly calls for a revision of the European Communities Act of 1972 and, further, of the Treaty of Rome itself. The demands put forward concerning Community policies are just as radical, since they more or less directly challenge the very idea of a common policy. This is the list: maintenance of the British Parliament's sovereignty in the conduct of economic and social policy, rejection of economic and monetary union which would lead to an increase in unemployment because of the economic discipline imposed (and thus opposition to the European Monetary System), dismantling of the common agricultural policy (through a more or less complete return to the system of deficiency payments, the abandoning of Community preference and a price-freeze). In short, it is a matter of achieving 'the creation of a larger and also much looser union of European States'.

But such demands do not have the support of the whole Labour movement. That they were put forward as the party's official position, with the distorting effect which that had on the debate itself, and the problems of evaluating it, was due to the fact that, contrary to normal practice in general elections, the drawing-up of the programme and the organisation of the campaign were monopolised by the extreme Left of the Labour Party, which has a majority within the Executive but represents only a quarter of the Parliamentary Party. In this way the campaign was dominated ideologically and in practice by the very anti-European figures of Tony Benn and John Silkin, the former Agriculture Minister. The pro-Europeans in the party were not amongst the speakers at the press conferences organised by Transport House, while those who held to the 'reformist' line, which supposedly rallies the whole party behind Mr Callaghan's European policy, did not participate in the debate as they should have done.

The position of the former Prime Minister gives an insight into the uncomfortable situation in which the Executive had placed the whole party: in order to preserve party unity, Mr Callaghan was forced to recommend a document which he had been unable to amend and the conclusions of which he did not share. During the press conference to launch the manifesto, where he appeared flanked by three well-known anti-Marketeers, he stressed his lack of involvement in the drafting of the document and refused to support the case for withdrawal from the EEC, claiming that, with a Conservative Government firmly established in power, the issue was irrelevant. Thus an analysis of the Labour Party's positions cannot be based merely on the visible tip of the iceberg. However, a comparison of the European manifesto with the programme defended a month earlier at the time of the general election would reveal a certain degree of bi-partisan convergence on European issues. This did not remove some important basic differences (for example, concerning the desirability of joining the EMS), but it did demonstrate the existence of a specifically British approach which was both pragmatic and defensive, both in its view of Europe and with regard to the development of its institutions and its policies.

The two major British parties shunned the flights of lyricism concerning Europe which frequently featured in the Continental debate. In relation to current difficulties and to the urgent measures which these call for, the past and future of the Community hardly seem to have supplied the British election campaign with its best issues. Obviously, thirty years of European unification, with all that that implies for peace and economic prosperity, have less significance for a country which has no common border with Germany and whose entry into the 'club', co-inciding as it did with a serious world crisis, has not brought it an economic 'miracle'. Rather than experiencing any positive attraction towards the European ideal, the British feel it is important not to be excluded from a Continental group sitting on their doorstep, so that they can influence its development. They are also conscious of the greater bargaining power which the EEC gives them in international negotiations, and of the advantages of diplomatic co-operation between the Nine.

In the institutional sphere one can even speak of consensus rather than convergence between the two major parties, since the Europe which they envisage is one of co-operation, not one of integration. The relatively limited debate which took place on the elections to the European Assembly is revealing in this respect. In fact, the election was not seen as a step towards supranationalism, but as an institutional redistribution which would weaken the Commission. They seem not even to have considered the possibility of an understanding between European Commission and the Assembly in opposition to the Council of Ministers, doubtless because of the belief, on the British side of the Channel, that direct elections would reinforce national allegiances.

If the word 'confederation' is never mentioned in Britain, this reflects the British mistrust of *a priori* constrictions and models; nevertheless any development towards such a form of federalism would be fiercely resisted. Only a Europe of the States in which real power is exercised by the European Council and the Council of Ministers is acceptable. From this point of view, the enlargement of the Community to include the candidate Mediterranean countries is welcomed by all the political forces, sometimes with ulterior motives which have nothing to do with strengthening the EEC. Without seeing it as the Labour Left does, as an opportunity to water down the Community into a vast and loose association of States soon to include the countries of Northern Europe also, enlargement is nevertheless seen as a brake on the development of an 'over-centralised and over-bureaucratised' Community (to use Mr Callaghan's phrase).

However, it should be emphasised that the issues which came up most frequently during the campaign had only a remote link with the event which produced it. Above all, the direct elections provided an opportunity for putting forward a programme of more or less radical reforms of Community policies, rather than a discussion about the present and future role and powers of the European Assembly. As the pro-European former Labour Minister Shirley Williams pointed out in the *Guardian* of 30 May, 1979:

> The major British political parties are walking vigorously backwards into the direct elections to the European Parliament, proclaiming all the things they will end, prevent or oppose.

This remark expresses the tone of an essentially defensive campaign in which there was more discussion about Britain in Europe than about Europe itself. Armed with reports about the former European Assembly, Conservatives and Labour competed with each other in their arguments and their oratory to assert from the outset that their respective Euro-deputies had been — and would be — the best defenders of the British people in Strasbourg. Indeed, this was what was promised in the slogans they adopted: 'The Labour Party will fight for you in Europe' and 'For a better deal in Europe, vote Conservative'. Since, for the purposes of the general election of 3 May, Mrs Thatcher had more or less adopted Mr Callaghan's policy of reforms, and thus occupied part of the ground held by the Labour Party, the list of policies

30

in need of reform scarcely differed from one party to the other. Basically, these were the issues which had dominated the membership negotiations: agricultural policy, the contribution to the Community budget, and fishing. Brought up to date, in 1979 these demands called first for a reduction of the budget contribution, considered to be out of all proportion to Britain's resources, and then for a reform of the agricultural policy which is a serious drain on the Community's finances. What this meant was, in particular, freezing the price of surplus foodstuffs, and some relaxation of the principle of Community preference. Finally, in fishing, the demand for exclusive and preferential zones for the British was supported by both parties.

At the height of the controversy, when the whole of France was up in arms, President Giscard d'Estaing, in a major speech on Europe (at Hoerdt, 15 May, 1979), chose to demonstrate the convergence of views held in French political circles. He went so far as to propose the formation of a French national group in the future Assembly, emphasising:

> Never has there been so wide a consensus about Europe in our country. No one, no one at all, is proposing to leave the Common Market. No one, no one at all, whether he voted for or against, is now proposing to amend the Treaty of Rome. That is the main point. The rest is merely detail and is not important enough to create deep divisions among Frenchmen.

This theme was developed by the Minister for Foreign Affairs and by the Prime Minister. It was supported by the Giscardians throughout the campaign.

The supporters of the Veil list were probably right in their view that, beyond all the party struggles, 'on the issue of Europe, what unites France is more important than what divides it'. However, contrary to what was suggested by the way they spoke, this unity was not built around a dynamic conception of the construction of Europe. It was based rather on a common determination to block this idea out of a fair number of developments, combined with one central preoccupation: the assertion of national independence. Moreover, it was the result of tactical concerns as much as of deep convictions.

The campaign's tone was set on 6 December, 1978 when Jacques Chirac launched his appeal from the Hôpital Cochin, where he was recovering from a car accident. He was resolutely nationalist. The leader of the RPR was to put the President of the Republic and his supporters on trial, unrelentingly accusing 'the foreign connection at work with its quiet and reassuring voice as always when France is being dragged down'. He pledged himself to fight against 'the supporters of self-denial and decline'.

The Communist Party, for its part, denounced the country's leaders who were not hesitating to

> draw on foreign support to work against the interests of the French people in the tradition of the Coblentz emigrés, of Thiers' alliance with Bismark against the Commune, or the Pétainist collaboration with Hitler . . . They want the important decisions about the life of our country and its inhabitants to be taken no longer in Paris, but in Brussels or Bonn. They want to see our national and regional cultures disappear and become standardised in the American mould. They want France, dismembered and weakened, to be integrated and drowned in

31

a West European conglomeration led by Federal Germany, and ultimately controlled by the United States.[1]

Faced with the attack led by Jacques Chirac and Michel Debré, President Giscard's supporters spent their time defusing the RPR's criticisms one by one, by constantly taking up their positions on the adversary's territory. Madame Veil took an essentially defensive stand. The traditional pro-Europeans remained in the background and only came forward to deny that they had ever been 'fanatical supporters of the supranational' (Jean Lecanuet, Radio Television Luxembourg, 28 April, 1979). Rather than adopting an aggressive posture and backing a pro-European programme, the tactic was to take up the RPR's nationalist themes as they occurred (even in the title given to the Veil list itself: Union for France in Europe) and to demonstrate how excessive Chirac's approach was, to what extent there was consensus on basic issues, and how current European policy was in direct line with that of General de Gaulle.

The Socialists, too, faced with the chauvinism of the Gaullists and the Communists, but also in response to certain CERES demands, paid tribute to nationalism. Less strongly, less often, in a more restrained way than the other political groups, but they did not escape.

Building Europe without destroying France, restoring to France her rôle in Europe, abiding by the obligations which we have contracted, but always fighting tooth and nail to defend French interests,

such were the conclusions of the Metz Congress in April.

The prominence given to domestic politics and the personalisation of the debate upset the situation so much that the slogans became interchangeable. 'Building Europe without destroying France' was just as much the theme of one of Michel Debré's meetings as the motto of the Socialists.

Each party took care not to be accused of sacrificing French interests to the European cause. It was this concern and these fears, for example, which prevented the whole serious issue of European defence from being openly debated before the electorate. On this taboo subject, all the political groups emulated each other's orthodox opinions in rejecting the idea of a common defence policy; the debate was only re-opened after the election. In addition, France was the only country in which the Community's involvement in financing the election campaign was challenged. At its first reading, and with an absolute majority, the National Assembly passed a Bill put down by the RPR, banning the political parties from receiving election funds through their European groups (art. 1) and preventing any organisation operating on French territory from making advertising contracts with the Communities concerning the European Assembly elections (art. 2). Although Parliament was divided on this matter[2], it should be pointed out that no one came forward to

---

[1]*For an independent France and a democratic Europe. Twenty proposals for Europe.* Manifesto adopted by the Central Committee of the PCF, 13 December, 1978.

[2]The Bill was passed by 246 votes to 124, with 485 voting. The 86 Communist deputies, the 150 (out of 155) RPR deputies and 10 independent deputies voted 'for'; the UDF (120 out of 122 deputies) voted 'against'. All the Socialists abstained.

speak against the Bill's basic objectives. Neither the Government nor the spokesman for the UDF gave any support to the view that an international organisation of which France was a member, and to which it made contributions, could not be considered as a 'foreign' organisation. Although the Socialists spoke against the first clause, this was because it was concerned with a persistent problem in French politics: the financing of political parties. What was even more significant was the quasi-unanimity with which almost all speakers saw information from the European Communities as an undue interference in French legal arrangements. The Government had to commit itself to contain the proposed information campaign 'within the strictest limits': under no circumstances should it 'constitute any interference whatsoever by the Community institutions in French affairs'. Rather than tackle the issue head-on, however, the matter was left to 'the wisdom of the National Assembly', and allowed to become caught up in red tape, with the result that the law did not get passed in time. No doubt when the next European election takes place the Bill will be brought out again. Aside from its economic and polemical aspects, the parliamentary debate on financing the election campaign confirmed the existence of an outstanding desire to reassert national independence against any kind of Community interference. Even amongst those who approached the election campaign with internationalist convictions, nationalist language prevailed over their commitment to Europe.[3]

Whether through a change of heart or through disillusionment, the cause of supranationalism has lost its supporters. No one today openly argues for an increase in the European Assembly's powers. To use President Giscard's own formulation of this institutional problem, 'all the legal barriers have been set up' (ie, the barriers against an extension of the Assembly's powers). Today, no one extols the virtues of building a federal Europe. The only list which openly campaigned for supranationalism, Jean-Jacques Servan-Schreiber's list ('Emploi, Egalité, Europe' — Employment, Equality, Europe), gained less than 2 per cent of the votes. The President of the Republic and his supporters came officially to support the Gaullist line on a confederal Europe. For both the UDF and the Socialist Party the keynote was 'The Treaty of Rome in its entirety, but nothing more than the Treaty'. All parties still hold that any revision of the Treaty of Rome must have unanimous support. Whether this is a fundamental belief or a matter of tactics, its influence is important. A force has been set in motion developing a general national 'consciousness' which could probably be mobilised to resist any infringement of national sovereignty by the Community.

Looking through the distorted images formed by the 'show-business' aspect of the campaign, one can also make out converging attitudes in certain specific spheres. With regard to the Common Agricultural Policy, everyone was agreed on maintaining the Community preference and financial inter-dependence, and on phasing out the Monetary Compensatory Amounts which penalise French farmers, even if

---

[3]'We do not wish a body external to our country to tip the scales on one side or the other. It is for each of us to develop our arguments and to make these known in a fair contest between French parties and organisations, without outside interference', Mitterrand stated. *Journal Officiel de l'Assemblée nationale*, 12 December, 1978, p. 9183.

evaluations of the policy and the remedies suggested differed from one political group to another. Moreover, the protection of the EEC's economic activities by the common customs tariff was a matter which featured to a greater or lesser degree in all the political platforms. François Mitterrand was united with Jacques Chirac and Michel Debré in deploring the fact that the Common Market was a 'sieve'. There was a consensus of opinion against dissolving the EEC into a larger free-trade zone. Although the parties tackled the political problem of EEC enlargement in different ways, in the economic sphere they all called for a long transition period, safeguard clauses, and protective measures for wine and those fruits and vegetables which are threatened by the prospect of Spanish and Portuguese membership.

Finally, two quite different issues stirred up emotions: on the one hand, unemployment, and on the other, West Germany's influence in the Community. On the first point, the maintenance of the Common Market was seen as a necessity, and no one called for withdrawal or complete self-sufficiency: but on the other hand, no one presented it as a source of hope. On the second, it seems that Germany has replaced the USA in French demonology. The obligatory diatribes against the Atlantic Alliance and American hegemony are largely things of the past. The campaign centred around Germany: the German model, Franco-German trade, German commercial supremacy, etc. The bitterness of these discussions made a curious contrast with the calmness of the campaign in West Germany itself.

In Federal Germany, party squabbles could not disguise the broad consensus between the parties, both on the need to unify Europe and on the way Europe should be organised. To be sure, the SPD had been severely critical of Konrad Adenauer's European policy in the 1950s, but it had come round to it completely during the early 1960s. Thus the consensus of 1979 represented an achievement which no politician thought of questioning. If the parties showed little partisanship on this point during the election campaign, it was because, as they all pointed out, the idea of elections to the European Assembly by direct universal suffrage had already been foreshadowed in the Treaty of Paris which set up the European Coal and Steel Community in 1951. The extension into the political sphere was thus merely an essential complement to achievements in the socio-economic sphere. The representatives of the three main political groups were unanimous in claiming that the limited nature of the European Parliament's powers, and the rather remote prospects of increasing these powers in the near future, was likely to deter voters. The subject of extending the powers of the Strasbourg Parliament was used more for tactical reasons than in the belief that this objective would be achieved quickly. In a State as federal in form as West Germany, the division of powers at different levels is an accepted fact of life, in contrast with the French experience which is based on excessive centralisation. Despite slightly different emphases, the German parties were thus united in their support for a political Europe, and all regretted that it was developing so slowly.

They were in agreement, too, in explaining to their voters that the many advantages which West Germany gained from the European Community fully justified their commitment to it. Since a few political facts were not sufficient to stimulate the electoral debate, the political leaders and the candidates, supported by the media, devoted themselves to demonstrating that West Germany and the EEC were made for each other. The same arguments, often interchangeable between one party and another, portrayed West Germany as a country which is geographically limited, with high population density and few raw materials and energy resources, and which is thus forced to play the export game in order to survive. It is as much through conviction as through necessity that West Germany supports a liberal concept of economic exchange, and relies upon the international division of labour as opposed to self-sufficiency, and upon the conciliation of interests rather than confrontation. The weakness of its agricultural sector, and the balance between industry and the other sectors, predispose it to involvement in Europe. West Germany's main trading partners are members of the EEC, and the German trade balance shows a deficit only with the Benelux countries and Italy. Does not the overall trade surplus between West Germany and its EEC partners enable it to obtain the currency which it needs to buy raw materials, notably oil, and thus to maintain its economic activity and prevent unemployment? Thus more than their European counterparts, the German parties emphasised the extent to which the EEC had helped to reduce the negative effects of the economic crisis which has been shaking the world in recent years. According to German statistics, which were widely quoted by the political groups, West Germany's European partners had only slightly decreased their imports from Germany, unlike the United States and Japan. The parties, both in the Government and in Opposition, were quite willing to enumerate the different forms of financial aid given by the EEC, particularly in the field of social affairs.

But the arguments in favour of the EEC could not hide the fairly harsh criticism made by all the parties about the bureaucracy in Brussels, the functioning of the Communities, and the resultant financial cost to West Germany. The EEC was a bottomless pit into which West Germany was pouring too much money. The Federal Government, worried by this rather demagogic argument, pointed out, however, that commercial advantages outweighed the expenses incurred by membership of the EEC. The Common Agricultural Policy, which takes up two-thirds of the European budget, was one of the critics' favourite targets, in so far as it leads to expensive over-production and to the artificial support of agricultural enterprises which are not really economically viable. But, again, during the campaign, the parties were brought round little by little to a more subtle approach to the agricultural problem. They were forced to admit that, for social reasons, a complete re-structuring of the agricultural sector was not possible, and that German farmers are the first to benefit from the EEC's higher prices. The sacrifices made for the benefit of agriculture were mostly off-set by the advantages gained in other areas of intra-European exchange.

All the parties expressed their concern that, far from diminishing, the divergence in economic strength within Europe was increasing, sometimes to the point of posing a threat to the Community.

It can be seen from this harmony of attitudes that, in Germany, unanimity between the parties led to ambitious but realistic expectations about the EEC. The politicians wished the Community to remain a force for economic and social development, to provide itself with stronger political structures, and to assert its role in world politics more clearly. It had to solve the immediate problems without neglecting all thoughts of the future. In West Germany there is a demand for faster and more complete implementation of common policies which too often have been held back by the crises of recent years: the return to monetary stability in Europe is regarded as a priority, provided that the battles against unemployment, inflation and the disparities in economic growth are not neglected. Consequently West Germany is concerned about the economic situation of its partners.

As in Germany, the absence of any debate on fundamental issues concerning the holding of the European election gave the Italian campaign a strongly united appearance. In the climate of generalised crisis which the country was experiencing, Europe appeared more than ever as the only possible framework in which these problems could be resolved. Thus all the ideas under discussion converged along the lines of strengthening European unity rather than retreating into nationalism. The adoption of the slogan 'A Government for Europe' on the eve of the election, and the constant and unanimous use of the term 'Parliament' to refer to the Assembly in Strasbourg, were indications of a general trend in Italian politics. All parties, including the Communist Party, were agreed on the two issues which were hotly debated in other countries: the extension of the powers of the European Assembly, and the enlargement of the Community to include the three Mediterranean countries seeking membership. On this last point in particular, there was no difficulty in reaching a unanimous decision. Indeed, this was dictated by the common belief that a restoration of the EEC's balance in favour of Southern Europe would enable Italy more successfully to put forward its own demands for the protection of Mediterranean produce, which until now had been neglected by its partners. It was this positive aspect which underlined the different party platforms, rather than the dangers of increased competition in certain important agricultural sectors, like wine, as in France.

An increase in the Assembly's powers, to counterbalance the omnipotence of the Council and the bureaucratisation of the Commission, was also put forward as a common demand for the democratisation of Community institutions; under this general agreement there were more or less committed attitudes on progress to supranationalism. Although the PCI saw the issue as above all about wider opportunities for initiating legislation, and the right to table amendments, some of the Christian Democrat and Republican candidates were anxious to see the Strasbourg Assembly become the Constituent Assembly of a Federal Europe.

All the parties agreed on a certain number of concrete proposals designed to ensure better protection of Italian interests in Europe, though again with varying degrees of intensity and often leading to different conclusions. Two issues dominated the election campaign: the South and agriculture, which of course are closely linked. Given that 17 of the 20 least developed regions in Europe are in Italy, all the candidates stated their support for an increase in the grants their country receives from the Regional and Social Funds, and for a decrease in the Italian contribution to the Community budget. For all of them, a genuine co-ordination of economic policies — which is a necessary condition for the success of the EMS — will come through an increased transfer of resources from the strong to the weak countries of the Community. They all believed this transfer could not be restricted merely to an increase in Community grants, but presupposed a revision of the Common Agricultural

Policy. There was immediate convergence of attitudes on the issue of abolishing the monetary compensatory amounts. This was not equally true for the basic problem: substituting a policy of transforming structures for a policy of price support. This was the major theme of the Communists' programme, which at all events was not opposed by the other parties' platforms.

The migration phenomenon supplied the candidates with a final common theme. The demand for a Code on migrant workers in the EEC, intended to halt the growth of the black market in manpower, and to provide Italian emigrants with increased welfare rights in their host countries, featured in most statements of policy.

Transnational dimensions
The organisation of the European Assembly along party lines and the prospect of its election by universal suffrage prompted the political parties to form transnational alliances. Only the British Conservatives and the candidates on the DIFE list acted alone. The Liberals, the Christian Democrats and the Socialists formed federations: the Federation of Liberal and Democratic Parties in the European Community, the European Peoples' Party, and the Confederation of Socialist Parties of the European Community. The Communist Parties, who did not join together to form a specific organisation, nevertheless increased their contacts and joint demonstrations.

The 'go-it-alones'
Since they constitute, with merely a few Danish Conservatives, the group of that name in the European Assembly, the British Conservatives were not limited by any transnational constraints during their campaign. As a result, they applied the same philosophy which had led them to victory on 3 May, advocating a reading of the Treaty of Rome which favoured economic liberalism and non-intervention by the State. The general tone was thus once again that of a 'crusade' against socialism, as exemplified, for example, in a campaign speech by the Secretary of State for Social Services, Patrick Jenkin. This statement specifically indicated that the European Parliament, in the Conservative view, faced exactly the same arguments as the British Parliament in relation to state interference, centralised regulation of the economy, levels of public spending, and policy on taxation. A powerful Conservative group in the European Parliament, he argued, would fight strongly for lower taxes, more choice, more competition and more liberty for individuals. Obviously such policies were prompted by distrust of the Commission's activities (regarding the development of regulations which was thought to be excessive, and the extension of industrial democracy), but they also gave a particular colour to Conservative proposals for reforming common policies.

It is significant that the reduction of Britain's contribution to the Community budget was sought through a decrease in expenditure on agriculture, and not by an increase in the amounts allocated to Britain through the Regional or Social Funds. Indeed a move in that direction would be out of line with the dogma on keeping down public expenditure.

In demanding a 'common sense' agricultural policy (this expression appears as a leitmotiv in their pronouncements), the Conservatives claimed that they were not calling into question the principle, but merely the errors of administration. They called for progressive devaluation of the Green Pound over five years, in order to allow British farmers a better competitive position, and a price-freeze for agricultural products which are in surplus, until such time as these surpluses could be eliminated. The disastrous consequences of this for 'inefficient' farmers should be off-set by assistance from national governments, since this constituted 'social' rather than 'agricultural' policy. Further, according to the manifesto, 'the common agricultural policy should be sufficiently flexible to allow the import of low-price foodstuffs, and the EEC should not try to exclude high quality Australian and New Zealand produce from our markets'. All this appeared difficult to reconcile with the principles of Community preference and financial solidarity, which are the basis of the Common Agricultural Policy, but did not stop the Conservatives from describing their approach to European affairs as 'positive'. This was claimed both with respect to continuity — the party's commitment to a united Europe — and to change, in relation to the Labour Party's European policy which was thought to be 'obstructive and malevolent'. Labour was criticised, for example, for not having joined the EMS. Since they supported it in principle, the Conservatives would seek ways of joining it.

Like the British Conservatives, the RPR conducted a purely national campaign, although it is part of the European Progressive Democrat Group, along with the Irish Fianna Fail and the small Danish Progress Party. Jacques Chirac's visit to Ireland in April 1979 resulted in more misunderstanding than agreement. In addition, the RPR is a member of the European Democratic Union which was set up in 1978 to counterbalance the Socialist International, on the initiative of the CDU-CSU, but meetings of the RPR's leader with the CDU have shown up the extent of their differences far more than they have promoted co-operation between the two movements, which are brough together by a single common concern: to prevent the Socialists and Communists from achieving power in Europe. Thus no European alliance developed to temper the Gallo-centred character of the DIFE programme, whose candidates had undertaken to form an independent group in the future Assembly, to provide 'a permanent counterbalance to the threats which the Brussels technocrats pose to the French economy through their excessive regulations'.

Apart from the issue of the Community institutions, which was taken up throughout the campaign, and the denunciation of the interference of the Commission and the Court of Justice, the RPR concerned itself mainly with four subjects: (i) the Common Agricultural Policy: any attempt to dismantle the CAP should be opposed, and the abolition of the monetary compensatory amounts, which distort the working of the agricultural common market and disadvantage French agriculture, should be achieved as a matter of urgency; (ii) the common customs tariff: 'If the Community does not react, it will cease to be an organised and protected market, and become increasingly a free trade area open to all the currents of international trade'; (iii) the industrial common market: in the key sectors, most of the European States were allowing themselves to be dominated by the United States and foreign multi-nationals: the Community had not played its proper role in the steel industry: the EMS was dangerous because it linked the franc with the progress of the mark, and thus French economic policy with German economic policy: 'The industrial common market leads to Euro-unemployment . . .

we do not accept that France should rely on European institutions which condemn us to under-employment'; (iv) the enlargement of the EEC to the South, on which the RPR expressed its fears — fear that an 'ill-considered integration' might threaten whole sectors of the French economy, particularly fishing and agriculture, fear that the Community 'which already functions with more difficulty with nine members than with six, might be completely paralysed with twelve, with greater proliferation of administrators and an intensified language problem'. Consequently 'this enlargement, which is desirable from a political point of view, should in no circumstances take place immediately so far as economic affairs are concerned, since the conditions are not yet right'.

The twenty-page brochure which the DIFE presented to the electorate thus dealt with subjects which, if seriously discussed, would have opened up to public debate some of the major issues of France's European policy. But the French were not given the opportunity to comprehend the importance of these serious technical and weighty subjects, which were lost in diatribe:

> This impotent Europe, this Europe which is open to all the world's crises like a sieve, this Europe which is not European but which is dominated by Germano-American interests, this Europe of imported unemployment, this spineless Europe which has no body and no real purpose, this Europe in which the multinational companies dictate their laws to the States, this Europe in which France will become bogged down as in a swamp, I say with calm determination, we will never accept this Europe. (Jacques Chirac, 31 March)

On the other hand, the anti-German flavour of the pre-campaign period in the spring of 1978 attracted more attention than the points which it was intended to make. The Gaullists did indeed defend themselves against the charge of being anti-Europeans, yet their campaign, in which one 'yes' was always followed by three 'nos', was understood as a rejection of the uniting of Europe.

The Liberals

In West Germany, in Italy, and in Britain, the Liberal Parties were alone in putting forward as their election platform the electoral programme of their European Federation. They had two aims in this: on the one hand, to show that they had long been the most 'European' of the parties, and on the other, to demonstrate their membership of a great transnational political movement, particularly because they represent only a marginal political force in their own countries. Their platform advocated a more balanced Community system, through an increase in the Assembly's powers, particularly with regard to the budget and legislation, and proposed that the Assembly should nominate the members of the Commission. The commitment to achieving economic and monetary union, beginning with a common currency, was the cornerstone on which 'liberal' economic integration, that is integration 'based on free enterprise and fair profits, but taking account of social needs, within the framework of a modern market economy', should be built. Further, the achievement of true economic union would require the harmonisation of social policies, public expenditure and taxation systems. Finally, special attention was paid to 'the citizens' Europe', and the newly elected European Assembly was thus called upon to draw up a kind of Charter of rights and liberties to this end, enabling individuals to petition the Court of Justice of the Communities even against their own national State.

Each party adapted this common programme to the overriding concerns of its own electorate. Thus the British Liberals emphasised the need to reform the agricultural policy, and to increase the Regional Fund's grants, in order to reduce Britain's contribution to the Community budget.

The two Italian parties which belong to the Federation (the Liberal Party and the Republican Party) hoped to see a truly capitalist system introduced in Italy to replace the one which they consider to be stifled simultaneously by Christian-Democratic populism and by the strength of the radical Left. This would imply restructuring the public sector, by making it subject to market forces, the 'end of the myth of taxation as the instrument of social justice', and stricter controls on trade union activity. Therefore, one of the European Assembly's tasks would be to put pressure on the Commission to regulate legislation to this effect. Even though this model was seen as 'germanisation', its adoption was deemed essential. In Germany, the FDP argued that progress towards European unity would promote the possibility of (German) reunification. However, its European programme also included ideas on nuclear energy (seen as dangerous and needing to be replaced by alternative forms of energy) and on economic policy (the development of flexible planning), which many of the FDP's leaders preferred not to defend publicly.

Paradoxically, however, the most important member of the liberal movement — the French Republican Party — dissociated itself from its European partners. In fact, just like the French Christian Democrats in the CDS (Social Democratic Centre), the French Liberals did not present themselves as such.

In drawing up the UDF's electoral platform, tactical considerations took precedence over European convictions, and in consequence, the transnational commitments made by its two main constituents, the PR and the CDS, were pushed into the background. The PR's national council, meeting to approve the party's European Charter on 13 February 1979, tacitly ignored previous policy statements favouring 'Liberal solidarity' and its membership of the Federation of Liberal Parties of the Community. Furthermore, one of its vice-presidents, Philippe Pontet, a UDF campaign organiser, emphasised the common ground between the PR and the European Socialist parties.

The document which all the parties and movements within the UDF accepted, and which became the programme of the Veil list, was presented by the Minister for Foreign Trade, Jean-François Deniau, on 12 December 1978: it was known as the 'Deniau report'. It gave firm backing for a confederal Europe, and for a limited definition of the powers of the European Assembly. It declared its support for the enlargement of the EEC, but subject to 'precautionary measures, gradual transition and special safeguards'.

A far cry from the Liberals' approach to the institutions, this report was even further removed from that of the European Peoples' Party. On the day when these proposals were made public, Jean Lecanuet, the leader of the CDS, originally a Christian-Democratic party and a component of the EPP, was attempting to reassure the German Christian Democrat leadership in Bonn.

The Christian-Democrats

The Social-Democratic Centre was in a particularly uncomfortable position. Under attack, because of their traditional and strongly pro-European views, from the combined forces of the Gaullists and the Communists against 'the foreign parties', the Social-Democrats had, in the words of one of their vice-presidents, 'to sacrifice themselves on the altar of the majority's policy, like the vestal virgins of ancient time. To sacrifice themselves so that the UDF might be alive now and in the future, at no matter what cost.' Presenting the 'Deniau report' to the political council of his party, Jacques Mallet, the CDS's general secretary for European affairs, expounded its philosophy as follows:

> The authors of the report were concerned to do three things: to avoid adopting positions which might divide the majority, or the UDF itself. The problem of European security has deliberately been left aside, and the problem of the European institutions has been approached with extreme caution. *This decision has sometimes led us to fall in line with the lowest common denominator: this is a non-sectarian programme which is not trying to make 'the most of Europe', but to attract the most votes* (UDF voters but also reasonable Gaullists or moderate Socialists); to place the programme within the context of the national interest; to promote concrete proposals which correspond to the current concerns of the French people, and which affect them in their daily lives.

Three weeks after adopting the proposals of the Deniau report (to which were added 'four fundamental principles of a European policy', which did not alter it at all), the CDS took part in the European Peoples' Party congress in Brussels, which brought together the Christian-Democratic parties of the Community (22-3 February, 1979). The electoral platform which was adopted at this congress took up themes which were already developed in the EPP's political programme drawn up in March 1978, and which was in complete contradiction to the programme which the members of the UDF had agreed to.

From its very first lines, the EPP's programme showed its 'desire to build a federal European Union in which everyone might feel at home'. It wished 'to reinforce the executive power of the Community, and to extend the jurisdiction of the European Parliament by amending the treaties'. It recommended 'within an appropriate period', but without conditions, the membership of Greece, Portugal and Spain. The EPP also stressed human rights and liberties, the demand for solidarity and justice and culture as the basis of European identity. In international terms, Europe was seen as an interdependent whole which had to prove its responsibility as much towards the Allies as towards the countries of Eastern Europe and of the Third World, or within international organisations like the United Nations. On the basis of what already existed, the EPP moved from a short general assessment of the EEC (a framework which guarantees liberty and asserts a real social dimension) to look at each sector in terms of the different common policies, trying to draw up a balance-sheet for each of them, and to outline future requirements. The EPP believed that, on the basis of the existing institutions, and with the European Assembly elected by universal suffrage, a genuine 'dynamic' would unfold. The

EPP's immediate aim was the formation of a 'united Europe' whose institutional forms were yet to be drawn up.

As a complement to the EPP programme, which was in any case strongly influenced by the CDU, the European programme adopted at Kiel at the end of March 1979 placed particular emphasis on economic matters. Reaffirming the principle of a social market economy, it condemned any trend towards the control of investments and restrictions on free enterprise. For its part, the CSU, in its Erlangen Manifesto, underlined the EPP's Christian and anti-Communist elements. More than the CDU, it stressed the role of political liberty as the fundamental value on which its European thinking was based, the principles of Christian ethics, the strengthening of Europe's defence capability, and close co-operation, on an equal footing, with the United States. Finally, the two German Christian Democratic parties emphasised the defence of human rights in Eastern Europe.

The Italian Christian-Democrats took three basic themes from the EPP platform: the Atlantic Alliance, European unification, and Christian co-operation. Everyone rejected the idea of a Europe mid-way between the United States and the USSR. Even the left of the Italian party, which is particularly sensitive to the problems of peace, détente and relations with the Third World, took every opportunity to point out that these aims are inseparable from security, and that security demands the existence of 'strong and lasting links – not only military ones – with the United States'. In addition, the Christian-Democrats saw the election of 10 June as a first step towards political and institutional integration. One of the party's distinguished candidates, Roberto Ducci, the ambassador in London, advocated that the Assembly should immediately assert its powers, for example opposing measures taken by the Council without its consent, and demanding a single permanent seat for the institutions of the Community. This attitude was shared by all shades of Christian-Democratic opinion. Luigi Macario, former general secretary of the Catholic trade union, the CISL, called for the Strasbourg Assembly to be transformed into a Constituent Assembly. Fundamentally the party in fact supports a federal rather than a confederal Europe. Finally, the Christian Democrats, the party of government par excellence, naturally had a close interest in the possibility of resolving, at European level, problems which they had been unable to deal with at national level: imbalances, whether regional (the South) or sectoral (agriculture), inflation, unemployment, etc. But they insisted on the ideological dimension of these choices. In asserting, for example, that 'Europe will remain merely an idea so long as a European in Hamburg has an income four times greater than that of a European in Calabria', there is not only a call for a more balanced and thus more rational development of Europe, but a reference to Christian responsibility. And thus one moves from the sphere of economics to the sphere of values. This was especially striking in the campaign of a man like Narducci, editor of the Catholic daily paper *l'Avvenire*, which was based on an opposition between an 'efficiency' model of the Scandinavian type, which had already revealed all its limitations, and the Christian 'ferment' model of the community idea, the outlines of which are drawn by the Church's social doctrines, modernised by Maritain's personalism (standing for Christian solidarism, pluralism, autonomy, defence of individual liberties).

The coincidence of the national and European elections led the Italian Christian Democrats to distance themselves somewhat from the EPP, however. Even in Brussels, when Leo Tindemans' statement emphasised economic difficulties and the establishment of a 'social market policy', the report by Benigno Zaccagnini, which was essentially *political*, stressed the need for democratisation and more popular participation, pluralism in Europe, and the free confrontation of all political forces. In presenting the party's programme in Milan on 12 May, Zaccagnini clearly stated that there were important differences among European Christian Democrats, and that the Italian DC's membership of the EPP in no way indicated that it intended to enclose itself within a restrictive framework, or that it wished to see a Europe controlled by Christian Democrats. In fact the Italian DC had nothing to gain from an assimilation with its German counterpart, which was dominated by its most conservative wing. Thus, with the exception of a Rome meeting of the EPP on 20 April, advertised with the slogan 'Together for a Europe of free men', joint events were carefully avoided. The paradox of the European elections originated in the fact that the DC's fear both of a compromising tête-à-tête with Strauss's Christian Democrats, and of the progressive transformation of the party into a classic European conservative party, was accompanied by a shift to the right, symbolised by the frequent recourse to anti-Communist themes, and by the predominance of unmistakably right-wing candidates (Scelba, Diana, Selva) on the electoral lists, whilst men like Prodi, the party's economics expert, or, even more striking, Granelli, one of the best-known, and one of the most left-wing, foreign affairs spokesmen, were not selected.

The Socialists
Unlike the other European groups, which did little campaigning together, the Confederation of Socialist Parties of the European Community organised a number of joint events. Six 'specialist conferences' were held in the various countries, and a meeting of socialist candidates in the European elections was organised in Luxemburg on 26 April. The end of the European campaign was marked by a big rally in Paris on 25 May, at which officials of the fourteen socialist parties were present, amongst them Willy Brandt, James Callaghan, Bettino Craxi and François Mitterrand.

The socialists' solidarity seemed more genuine than in earlier years. Of course, it had not been possible to agree on a united platform, and the parties were free to uphold their own programmes. But a joint declaration was published in Brussels on 24 June 1978. The French PS achieved its purpose on two points: the demand for 'an appropriate timetable of transitional periods' for the enlargement of the Community, and the clause according to which 'any further transfer of powers from national governments to the Community institutions or from national parliaments to the European Assembly can take place only with the clear and direct assent of the national governments and parliaments'. Furthermore, the 10th Congress of the Confederation of Socialist Parties (Brussels, 10-12 January 1979) succeeded in unanimously adopting an 'appeal to the electorate' which went much further than the Brussels declaration. It stated

In shaping this European Community, the logic of the capitalist market system —

namely the pursuit of private commercial and financial interests — has for too long prevailed over the search for commonly defined social and human objectives. Unemployment results from the crisis of the present economic system . . . The market economy will not lead automatically to social justice.

The appeal advocated a new economic policy. 'The conventional economic policy instruments have proved inadequate: an active employment policy and the planning of the economy will be necessary to redirect growth towards more social objectives, and to reduce unemployment.' It took as its aim keeping Europe's economic and social development under 'democratic control': democratisation of industry at all levels, public control of big industrial and financial concentrations, multinational companies, etc.

Despite these notable rapprochements in the direction of anti-capitalism and the 'Europe will be socialist or will not be at all' argument, many points of disagreement remained, however, some of which made the headlines.

The Manifesto adopted by the Labour Party Executive, for example, rarely reflected the letter, and still less the spirit, of the Brussels 'Appeal', which Labour had nevertheless signed. It was not so much its attitude to the unification of Europe as the conclusions which it drew from it, which separated the Labour Left from the European socialists. Although Tony Benn shared the view of certain Continental socialists that 'the heart of our objection is that the Common Market is based on a written constitution in which the principles of capitalism are entrenched', he felt that an essential priority was the revision of the Treaty of Rome, stripping the Commission and the Court of Justice of their powers in order to enable national governments to exercise 'democratic control over the economy'. Consequently co-operation with sister parties was called for, mainly to endorse the views of the Labour Party Executive. For although it was admitted that socialism cannot be confined within national boundaries, it was its British version which the Manifesto proposed to adopt:

> The policies we advocate are relevant, not only to Britain but to Socialists in all the EEC Member States, and we are therefore sure that they will be taken up by the Socialist Parties throughout the Community. We will work closely with like-minded parties and with the trade unions towards a policy of joint action on all parts of our programme.[4]

In fact, all references to co-operation with the European socialists were effectively erased from the campaign, and membership of the Confederation of Socialist Parties was only mentioned for tactical purposes to emphasise the isolation of the Conservatives in Strasbourg. More fundamentally, the Labour Left did not really give precedence to the European dimension over wider international alliances. But coherent as this statement might be, with its implicit preference for withdrawal from the EEC or for watering it down into a loose association of states, it only represented — as we have seen already — a fraction of the Labour movement.

---

[4]*European Assembly Elections* (Manifesto adopted by the National Executive Committee of the Labour Party) pp. 10-11.

To be sure, Callaghan did his best to maintain the minimum contact with the European socialist leaders during the campaign. But within the party, the social-democrats remained almost silent. Yet they would have been able to show, as did Shirley Williams, 'the ambivalence of the Community philosophy' and the prospects opened up by the Treaty of Rome, the spirit, if not the letter, of which favours the adoption of Welfare-State-type policies. Thus, the moderates within the Labour Party distanced themselves from a transnational debate which involved them, and to which they could have made a positive contribution.

For the parties in the other three countries, on the other hand, the European socialist alliance was a major element in their electoral strategy. François Mitterand expressed a common conviction when he stated: 'Together, the socialist and social-democratic parties represent the most powerful workers' movement, and the most powerful current of opinion in the Europe of the Nine'. The importance accorded to this solidarity meant that differences which might exist between, or even within, each of the various parties were minimised. The continuing debate which divides the French PS, for example, on the advisability of joint activities with the SPD, which was very lively during the pre-election period, was temporarily relegated to a secondary level for the duration of the campaign. François Mitterrand came to the fore, Pierre Mauroy and Michel Rocard remained back-stage, and the CERES agreed to suspend its criticism of the party's 'drift towards the Atlantic Alliance' for the time being. Also, despite the internal battles which were tearing the PS apart at the same time, despite the disagreements on the advisability of forming a joint list with the Left Radicals, despite the old divisions on Europe, the Socialist Party presented a united front during the campaign, around the 'Socialist Manifesto for the European election', adopted by the steering committee on 21 October 1978, and the motion passed by the party's congress in Metz on 8 April 1979.

Unlike the Liberal, Christian Democrat and Conservative parties, the socialists joined together to stress the need to transform the Community. However, if all were agreed about converting the 'Europe of the multinationals' into a 'workers' Europe', profound differences emerged as to the degree and the form of this change, whether on its socio-economic content, on the Community institutions, or on Europe's role in the world. As a Government party in a country where the importance of the Communists is negligible, the SPD is naturally tempted to go less far than its partners along the road to change. The French PS, on the contrary, the main opposition party, which remained faithful to the strategy of left-wing unity, defended the most radical positions. The Italian Socialists, already divided into two camps (PSDI and PSI), sometimes came close to the SPD and sometimes the PS, according to the subject under discussion and the factions which supported them.

Only the French party, strongly influenced by the CERES, made a clear call for a break with capitalism. Objecting to the Common Market as it stands, that is, 'dominated by big capital', it condemned the liberal approach on which the Treaty of Rome is based. Putting forward its proposals for building 'another Europe', it stressed, unlike the German Social Democrats, the different paths which are possible for the achievement of economic democracy, above all, democratic planning processes at Community level, self-management and workers' control.

45

Similar views were upheld by the left-wing of the Italian Socialist Party, which raised the important issue of correcting market forces through a common programme, which would set the targets for balanced growth. On the fundamental question for Italy of the inequality of regional development, some Socialists, like Giorgio Ruffolo or Mario Zagari, questioned the policy which the EEC had followed up to now, based on the requirements of a capitalist society, and which had intensified, rather than alleviated, the differences between rich and poor areas. But, as a whole, the PSI placed hardly any emphasis on the two basic elements of a truly socialist programme: economic planning and the role of public enterprises. Indeed, this was an area where it was difficult to find any common ground between the Italians and the Germans, common ground which was the linchpin of the party's strategy.

The left wing of the SPD carried its hopes for a socialist, and not merely social-democratic, Europe through to European level. The German Christian Democrats and the liberal press immediately saw in this stance a dangerous rapprochement with the Marxist approach. The SPD supported an essentially reformist interpretation of the Treaty of Rome and the Community, advocating some specific alterations within the framework of the existing system, whilst at the same time endeavouring to refute the view widely held outside Germany, according to which the SPD was merely a tool of modern capitalism.

But, whatever their analyses, the socialist parties of the three countries were convinced that only a concerted response, at European level, could bring about solutions to the most alarming problems, especially the problem of employment, which was a priority everywhere. Thus they again found themselves united on common demands (the 35-hour week, control over the multinationals by the European institutions), and they all upheld the need for united action by the labour movement (negotiation of collective agreements and the possibility of pursuing conflicts at European level). In this respect the European Trade Union Confederation's congress in Munich in May 1979 attracted the attention of the socialist parties, especially of the PSI which made extensive use of the resolutions adopted by the Confederation in its campaign.

Foreign policy was a minor issue in the campaigns of all the socialist parties: in France and Italy because of deep divisions within the parties, and in West Germany because it seemed to be outside the party's immediate concerns. Although, for the French socialists, Europe was 'a decisive continent' for the development of major world conflicts, 'the pivot of a possible rethinking of East-West and North-South relations', and although they believed that Europe was 'the only means of becoming an agent of change on the world scene', the conclusions which they drew from this in foreign policy remained vague. The political co-operation of the Nine had to be shaped independently of the great power blocs, and Europe had to assert itself as a powerful element in détente, disarmament and peace. Europe was still first and foremost the home of human rights and of liberty, and no discrimination, no abuse of power, including in the economic sphere, should be tolerated. The French Socialist manifesto for the European elections ended:

Today, the Socialists are opposed to Giscard's liberalism and to his view of the world, in which sham Europeanism and sham internationalism with increasing difficulty conceal the acceptance for France of the place of a second-rate vassal, in an American empire whose functioning and ultimate objectives are not questioned.

In Italy, apart from the issue of human rights, which stirred the whole party, as evidenced by Pelikan's candidature, the range of Socialist proposals was very wide. The speeches of two equally important PSI personalities, Giolitti and Signorile, were significant in this respect. The former explained that the party had long ago chosen its side, Western Europe, and that any attitude half-way between 'the values of liberty, democracy and social justice which characterise the western left wing parties, and the values upheld by the Communist dictatorships' was alien to the policy of the PSI. The latter spoke of an autonomous Europe which could not be 'a mere appendage of American policy' but which, spurred on by the Socialists, would be able to develop an 'original and realistic policy', particularly on the Mediterranean and on Africa. This demand for European autonomy would, of course, not lead to the creation of a third power, but to the transformation of the international system, still substantially dominated by the superpowers, into a multipolar system based on 'economic co-operation, social development, détente, the control and limitation of armaments, and solidarity with the Third World' (Mario Zagari, *Avanti*, 20 May 1979). It is clear that such an approach is close to that of the PCI, but is not one shared by the whole of the Socialist Party.

The SPD saw the European Community as a model for co-operation between states on equal terms, not dominated by any one state and especially not by West Germany. Without questioning the close links with the United States, the SPD firmly stressed relations with Eastern Europe. Better co-operation with the 'other' Europe would help to overcome the present divisions, starting with those of Berlin and Germany. West Germany would be in a good position to make the link between the two Europes. Thus the SPD saw the European Community's mission as an essentially peaceful one.

The French, German and Italian socialist parties accepted the European institutions and saw the Assembly as a forum for major campaigns uniting all workers in the EEC behind joint social demands, as well as an instrument of popular control over bureaucratic decisions. But the French PS set itself apart from its partners by being the only one to refuse to support an increase in the Assembly's powers, or reducing the powers of the national governments. In addition, the PS had 'decided that the French government should establish procedures for informing and consulting with Parliament before taking any important decision'. Mitterrand's reply to those who disagreed with him, and who turned to the statements of Helmut Schmidt and Willy Brandt to oppose him on this point, was that 'supranationals can be found everywhere', particularly in the PCI, but that, as the Assembly had no power to amend the treaties, these fears were unfounded. For the PS the supranationality issue was a 'false issue', a 'false debate'. The 'real problem' was that of the enlargement of the Common Market. In this connection the PS drew attention to the basic principles which it upholds concerning the Common Agricultural Policy, and which separate it from its German and British partners: the abolition of monetary compensatory amounts, the organisation of markets for the products affected by enlargement (wine, fruit and vegetables) and the application of a system of minimum prices regulated at the frontiers in the official currency of the importing country, the establishment of offices for the various products, which would have regulating mechanisms to permit differentiation between producers, and a more equitable distribution of income. As the campaign progressed, however, the national theme slipped gradually into the background, while the essential element of the PS's electoral strategy took shape: the alliance with the German Social Democrats. Increasingly, François Mitterrand was persuaded to erase the differences between the French Socialists and the Social Democrats, to enable him to claim that 'that which unites us is stronger than that which divides us'. The accusation, made by the PCF for tactical reasons, that there was a rapprochement between Socialists and Giscardians, via the intermediary of the Social Democrats, and also the numerous references made by the UDF to social democracy, led the Socialist Party to defend Chancellor Schmidt and the Germans SPD against 'the official propaganda' which was attempting to link them with the French Right. Mitterrand's simple remark, 'Herr Schmidt is on the Left', was much commented upon, and the PS's statements (cf Claude Estier's article in *L'Unité* 25 May-1 June 1979) were seen as something of a hymn in praise of the SPD.

The Communists

In comparison with the big Christian Democratic, Liberal and Socialist federations, the Communist Parties of the EEC had no similar organisation as a point of reference. The differences which divided the two most important of them, the PCF and the PCI, on basic aspects of the European programme, such as the strengthening of the Assembly's powers and the enlargement of the Common Market, had brought them during their meeting in Brussels on 24 September 1978 to the point of 'excluding any common European programme, which would be inconsistent with the principle of independence, to which they were unanimously committed'. The idea was expressed even more bluntly by the PCF, when it stated that it did not wish 'to form links with foreign programmes and parties, unlike the other French political parties'.

Since their joint opposition to European unification in the 1950s, the positions of the Italian and French Communists have diverged rapidly. Coming more quickly and more completely, the PCI's change of heart gave it a reputation for 'Europeanism' and openness, which can easily be contrasted with the PCF's nationalistic sectarianism. In fact, they are in agreement on many matters, and especially in their judgment of Europe as it stands. For the PCF, the record is disastrous: 'Seven million unemployed, an economy in its death-throes, an agricultural crisis, the dismantling of branches of industry such as coal and steel, factory closures, dying regions; this is their Europe, the Europe of the Right and of social-democracy' (document of 13 December 1978). The PCI's indictment of Europe at the present time echoes this entirely negative assessment: Europe is seen as the Italians' 'wicked step-mother', because of their Government's subordination to the big capitalist organisations in the strongest countries. A catalogue of disasters is listed in the various spheres. The PCI explained to emigrant workers that they were not 'treated as Europeans' but as 'workers who are more exploited than other workers'; to the farmers that the common policy had benefited agriculture in the rich countries at their expense; to the southerners that they were doubly penalised by European policy, both as migrant workers and as farmers.

In another connection, the absolute priority given to the subject of détente, co-operation and arms limitation in the PCI's campaign was exactly in line with the concerns of the international Communist movement. Their praise of the Helsinki Conference and of Salt II, and their fear of a reversal of the trend towards ever wider détente between East and West, which were the leitmotivs of the Communist campaign, are better understood within the framework of the Italian party's own strategy. Clearly it is more difficult to follow a national road to socialism in a climate of international tension. But these issues also arose out of a concern for solidarity with the Soviet Union. In this respect the French Communist Party also had no option but to approve of them, even though it had given a limited priority to foreign policy considerations, which were relegated to nineteenth place in its 'twenty proposals for Europe'.

It is not possible, then, to interpret the two parties' willingness to co-operate and re-establish their links as merely a contrived piece of publicity and propaganda. The two joint meetings held in Marseilles and then in Turin (19-21 May 1979) provided an opportunity to underline their agreement on the general objective: to guide the Community in the direction of workers' interests, democracy, peace and co-operation between sovereign States.

Their differences were none the less real. They had to do with a fundamental issue: their analysis of the present crisis, and of related issues such as what responses the labour movement should make, whether European or national, negotiated with or without the social democrats of Northern Europe.

For the PCI, the economic crisis which Italy is experiencing cannot be understood merely as the result of bad management by a moderate government, but as a manifestation of the general crisis of the Welfare State. In a world in which problems have become increasingly international, and in which the inappropriateness of neo-liberal Keynesian-type solutions is provoking a resurgence of conservative, and sometimes plainly reactionary, forces everywhere, the Italian Communist leaders see Europe as the true battleground of the working class and the trade union movement. For Enrico Berlinguer, it is not only that 'taken individually the different European States are too small to confront the new problems, and the weakest ones are relegated to a subordinate position in relation to the great powers if they act alone', but also that it is necessary for the working class to offer a more unified response to the international co-operation between the employers and the moderate political forces. In this respect the events of the European Trade Union Confederation's congress in Munich in May 1979 provided the PCI with significant support for its analogy between the problems facing European workers and the need for a common strategy. The PCI welcomed decisions such as that on joint action on reducing working hours (which it would be impossible to apply in a single country) or the even more radical one on organising joint campaigns, as a major step towards the unity of the European working class, despite the ideological differences between the trade unions.

The PCF saw the same congress as one of 'limited sovereignty' for the unions. According to Georges Séguy, the congress came 'within the logic of the European integration policy which the German Social Democratic Party, of which Heinz-Otto Vetter is one of the leaders, wishes to force the entire West European trade union movement to adopt'. Georges Frischmann, a candidate on the Communist list, declared that 'its purpose indeed is to provide at European level the necessary link between the supranational political authority of the future and the European Trade Union Confederation, which itself has supranational powers, for imposing an entire policy which is against the workers' interests' (*L'Humanité*, 16 May 1979).

Unlike the PCI, the PCF interprets the crisis as 'above all a national crisis. In order to escape from it, and to achieve the 'democratic self-managed socialism' which would break capital's total domination of the State and the economy, the PCF at its 23rd Congress re-asserted that the nation State 'formed the most suitable framework for achieving a political situation favourable to the satisfaction of the needs of the French people, and to the transition to socialism'.

No longer constrained by the Union of the Left, which had caused it to make concessions on Europe in the 'Common Programme' of 1972, the PCF resumed its class analysis of the Common Market: in the world strategy of imperialism, European integration under West German control was an objective supported by the United States. It represented a division of labour between the forces of big capital, multinational companies and capitalist powers, 'a veritable strategy for the decline of France'. The results of such a policy were currently disastrous, and were creating 'a France which would be dependent, disjointed, sub-contracted, underdeveloped in certain fields, a France which had become a secondary province of an Empire whose Charlemagne would be a German'. Anti-German feeling was, in fact, the logical consequence of this analysis. It was a daily element in the PCF's campaign, and on occasion took an extreme form during the demonstrations provoked by the steel crisis ('1870, 1914, 1940, 1979, enough'). From its diatribe against German capitalism, which, according to Georges Marchais, 'hopes to achieve through the European institutions what it was unable to gain during two world wars', the PCF moved easily to an attack on social-democracy. In a style hardly given to understatement, this criticism of a political movement, accused of organising 'the unrestrained domination of the multinational companies' and 'the exploitation of workers and peoples', included both 'the Giscard-Schmidt tandem' and the French Socialist Party.

The PCI, on the other hand, has always — even at the height of the Eurocommunism period — tried to establish close relationships with the Socialist and Social Democratic forces of Northern Europe in as much as they are the only representatives of the working class in these countries. During the months leading up to the European elections, contacts were increased, mainly with the German Social Democrats because of the anti-European views held by part of the British Labour Party and the desire to avoid involvement in the quarrels of the French Left. In the absence of any Communist organisation at European level, and faced with the general rise in right-wing movements, it seemed doubly necessary to ensure a rapprochement of the two separate elements of the European labour movement. Only in this way could the Left regain its strength and its ability to act in a Europe where, acting alone, Social Democrats in Great Britain as well as in Germany have been forced to abandon their plans for imposing sweeping reforms, and to content themselves with 'crisis management'. The PCI's attitude towards the Social Democrats, especially the SPD, is in fact by no means uniformly one of good-will. The Italian Communists reject the 'German model' to which the SPD is committed, in both its economic and its political aspects. The ideological differences between the PCI, which remains a 'revolutionary' party, that is, with the ultimate objective of a radical transformation of social relations, and the Social Democrats are clearly underlined. It was amusing, however, to see Berlinguer, at the very moment when he was trying to reach an agreement between the PCI and the SPD, at the European Assembly, strongly criticising Craxi for having broken with the tradition of Italian socialism, by aligning the ideological and political positions of the PSI with those of the European Social Democrats.

Thus the insistence of the Communist election campaign on the issue of relations with the Social Democrats conceals a fairly deep uncertainty in the PCI's strategy on the issue of class alliances, owing to both the transference of domestic uncertainties to the European scene and the ambiguity of the German problem. One of the reasons which drove the PCI, unlike the PCF, to refrain from engaging in polemical discussions about Chancellor Schmidt, was the need to encourage the SPD in its fight against German Christian Democracy, the target of all the PCI's attacks ('To abstain is to give support to Strauss and conservative Europe', a slogan proclaimed just before the elections). External concerns, more important than at first appeared, were not irrelevant to these policy statements, including in particular the requirements of the Ostpolitik. Thus while Marchais saw Schmidt as the most effective tool of American policy for an anti-Soviet Europe, Berlinguer considered Brandt as the guarantor of a Community policy which would not upset the USSR. More fundamentally, one of the reasons for seeking agreement with the SPD was the importance which the PCI attaches to rapprochement between the two Germanies (for which the SPD is the only channel) as a factor in the development both of Eastern and of Western Europe.

Here, with the definition of Europe's place in world affairs and especially in East-West relations, we find one of the major issues of the Communist campaign. The PCI, as much as the PCF, showed it was concerned about European autonomy: 'What we must avoid at all costs', stated Pajetta, 'is becoming tenants in a building where the owner lives in Washington, and the first floor is occupied by the multinationals'. But the two parties drew radically different conclusions. For the PCF, the strengthening of the Assembly's powers and the enlargement of the EEC were synonymous with 'national surrender, social decline, and the destruction of the productive capacity of agriculture, indeed of the whole French economy'. For the Italian Communists, the direct elections to the Assembly and the strengthening of its powers were a guarantee of greater autonomy vis à vis the influence of the United States: the PCF was directly challenged by the Paris correspondent of *l'Unità* for being 'committed to turning the Assembly into a powerless body, with no means of controlling the executive, which will thus continue its activities in favour of the big multinational economic forces', and for having 'declared itself against any enlargement of the Community, in the name of the interests of vine-growers in the South of France, Breton fishermen or steelworkers in Lorraine,' in the worst tradition 'of the corporatist nature of a divided society'.

Most of the analyses concerning the first European election by direct universal suffrage take particular account of its significance for the political 'families', since, quite obviously, the future of an efficient European Assembly depends on their ability to form genuine and homogeneous political movements. In fact, as one might have expected, the election demonstrated the predominance of tactical considerations, sectoral interests and national issues, whilst the gap between the speeches and the traditional preferences distorted matters still further. Although coloured by a transnational dimension, the campaign tended to bring out the explicit or diffuse convergences which went beyond or contradicted the party alliances, whether it was a matter of how the Community institutions should develop, of socio-economic choices, or of Europe's place in world affairs.

Obviously the national parties are not yet ready to change into European parties, and this will probably neither allow the Strasbourg Assembly to penetrate the Council's prerogatives nor modify the development of a unified Europe based on intergovernmental co-operation. In this respect the campaign brought out the instability of the alliances being made and broken between the States in relation to basic or circumstantial choices: between the defenders of free trade and their more interventionist partners, between contributors to and beneficiaries of Community funds, between producers and consumers of agricultural goods, between supporters of some degree of supranationalism and upholders of national sovereignty, between the faithful supporters of a European Europe and the supporters of a larger Atlantic entity.

Nevertheless this last division seemed to be much less deep than in the past. In comparison with previous 'European' debates, the election was in fact notable for the relative absence of the United States. Of course no-one questioned the Western alliance, but the troubles of the dollar and US problems both at home and abroad led to a certain distancing from Washington. For example, one of the most prominent Euro-candidates, Sir Fred Catherwood, declared in London during the campaign, 'The power of America is no longer what it was . . . the Western end of the great democratic alliance is in decline, and the European end has to begin to bear its full share as it should'.

This distancing from the United States certainly provides proof of an awareness of European identity. But too many obstacles still remain for all the logical conclusions to be drawn: the absence during the campaign of any serious debate on a defence policy for Europe is revealing in this respect.

IV The 'Dear Europeans' and the Uneasy People

Opening the first session of the European Assembly, Louise Weiss challenged the newly-elected representatives with an irony tinged with sadness: 'My dear Europeans, you must admit that your election campaigns have often seemed more concerned with ulterior motives of a party political nature than with European considerations . . .'

Was it really the prevalence of such ulterior motives which made Europe so unattractive that in every country the electorate became bored with the campaign to the point of saturation?

In Britain and Italy the holding of national elections a few weeks or a few days before the European poll had exhausted both the activists' energy and the parties' coffers. In no country was the election of 81 representatives to the Assembly in Strasbourg seen as a decisive event by a population struggling with the daily problems of inflation and unemployment. Even in a country where European feeling is strong, like Italy, the PCI, which had mounted a huge information campaign, holding meetings in its branches and districts, admitted that it came up against ignorance and general apathy. In France, as in Germany, there was a striking contrast between the overall quality of the studies and documents prepared for the campaign by the various political groups and the mediocrity of the debates, which did not produce a single political proposal capable of arousing public interest. In three of the four countries considered here, opinion polls confirmed that a general openness towards Europe co-existed with a low level of information about and lack of serious interest in the election. This comes over clearly in the table.

In Britain, both the politicians and the majority of the electorate would willingly have foregone another election. The start of the official campaign, on 9 May, passed virtually unnoticed; for example, the parties only presented their European manifestos at a much later date. Although certain newspapers such as the *Financial Times* and the *Guardian* tried to alert public opinion to the election, by providing information about the issues at stake and what was happening in the other European countries, it never reached the headlines of the popular press. There was no radio or television coverage on a scale comparable with coverage in France. One had to wait until the last few days of the campaign, when there were the party political broadcasts and some 'phone-in' programmes, before one became aware of how close the election was.

	Italy	West Germany	France
		Percentages	
Percentage who mentioned the European election spontaneously	60	46	38
Percentage claiming to have been aware of the publicity campaign about the European election.............................	72	50	47
Respondents:			
'Very pro-' or 'fairly pro-'.................	87	82	72
'fairly anti-' or 'very anti-'	4	7	10
For the respondent's country, EEC membership is:			
A good thing	78	66	56
A bad thing	2	5	8

Source: Opinion poll conducted on behalf of the European Community in April 1979 (*Euro-Baromètre* No. 11). Percentages in each line do not add to 100 because non-responses are not included in the table.

And yet, the British public needed information about this election more than any of the others: in October 1978 an opinion poll conducted on behalf of the EEC Commission found that 44 per cent of British people had 'read or heard something about the European Parliament', but that only 18 per cent 'were able to say that it was about the election'. These figures increased to 55 and 25 per cent respectively in April 1979, but nevertheless remained the lowest in all the Nine member countries.[1]

The turn-out
Compared with the other three major countries in the Community, Italy can be proud of its exceptionally high turn-out: 85.9 per cent of the electorate. By Italian standards, however, this represented a considerable reduction in public involvement, a phenomenon already present in the legislative election of 3 June (albeit to a smaller degree).

On 10 June, abstentions and spoilt papers followed different trends. The number of abstentions increased (a million and a half up on 3 June), while there were almost a third fewer spoilt and unmarked papers. This leads one to believe that the explanation must be different from that given at the time of the national election. It was more political in the case of the Italian parliamentary election, expressing a

---

[1]*Eurobaromètre* No. 11, May 1979. See also the data and commentary in R. Inglehart and J.R. Rabier, 'L'élection du Parlement européen: aptitudes individuelles à participer et mobilisation collective de l'électorat', *Rapport présenté au XIe congrès mondial de l'A.I.S.P.*, Moscow, 12-18 August 1979, p.6.

general rejection of the party system; in the case of the European election, the phenomenon was the result of less direct interest and of technical difficulties, particularly for emigrants. The regional distribution of the abstentions confirms these explanations. Abstentions were particularly high in the South — on average 80 per cent of the electorate voted (78.8 per cent in Naples) — a region which has both a high level of emigration and less sensitivity to European problems. They were low in the 'red' areas — about 93 per cent of the electorate voted in Tuscany and Emilia — where there are acute social pressures, and in the industrial North — 91.5 per cent in Piedmont, 90 per cent in Milan — where there is a strong awareness of the European Community. The southern electoral districts were also those where there were most spoilt papers — 4.8 per cent in the fifth district, reaching as high as 10 per cent in Messina and 8.5 per cent in Cagliari. It is worth remarking that the percentages were roughly the same in the first district — 4.5 per cent spoilt papers, rising to 10 per cent in Turin. Only a very detailed analysis could show whether this protest behaviour was specifically directed at Europe as it is understood by a population which has both direct and indirect experience of the suffering caused by emigration (one must take account of the southern population in Turin), or whether it was directed at the domestic policies of the various political parties.

In West Germany, the turn-out, higher than expected (65.9 per cent), came as a surprise. It was much lower, however, than in the federal elections of 1976 (90.7 per cent). In comparison with 1976, 10 million electors failed to vote. Each of the two major parties lost 4-6 million votes compared with 1976, and the FDP lost 1-3 million. As Egon Bahr remarked while the votes were being counted, the abstainers and the ecologists alone accounted for one third of the electorate. The percentage of spoilt papers (0.9 per cent) was identical with that in the 1976 federal elections.

In France the high abstention rate — 39.29 per cent — was similar to that which led Georges Pompidou, in 1972, to regard the low poll in the referendum on enlarging the Common Market (39.75 per cent abstained) as a personal failure. In contrast with the 1972 poll, when the Socialist Party called on its supporters not to vote, in 1979 only the smallest political groups (Gaullistes d'opposition, Front national, Parti Socialiste Unifié) advocated abstention or spoiling the ballot. Although there was a 23 per cent increase in votes not cast, compared with the 1978 elections, there was no advantage for any political party in the exceptional number of abstentions and spoilt papers.

If one compares the French electorate's turn-out in the European elections with their massive vote either in the March 1978 legislative elections (16.68 per cent abstentions in the first round) or in the 1974 presidential elections (15.7 per cent abstentions in the first round), the abstentions in the 10 June elections at first seem to indicate a defeat for Europe. Yet the geographical distribution of abstentions varied only slightly from that in the national elections. In the industrial regions, the increase in abstentions in Lorraine, for example, was off-set by the record poll in Nord-Pas-de-Calais; in the South West, where the problem of the enlargement of the Community was an issue, the generally good turn-out (around 64 per cent) was lower in Languedoc-Roussillon (59.6 per cent). In Strasbourg itself, only 53 per cent of the electorate voted, despite great efforts by the press and all the political parties in the area to sensitise public opinion. In an over-dramatised election, but one which was not concerned with choosing a 'new kind of society', the politicians' games failed to attract votes, and what was at stake in Europe left the electorate unmoved.

Abstention was the main feature of the election in Britain, where it was higher by far than in the other countries of the Community. In fact the turn-out was 33 per cent and even this figure would not have been achieved without the higher poll in Northern Ireland, where it reached 57 per cent. Without the Irish vote, the turn-out in Great Britain drops to 32.6 per cent. The difference in relation to the general election on 3 May was considerable: 76 per cent of the electorate voted on that occasion (for comparative purposes, there was a 72.8 per cent turn-out in the 1974 election and a 64.5 per cent turn-out in the June 1975 referendum on membership of the EEC), which shows that the high level of abstention on 10 June was not part of a general trend towards low polls.

At first sight, abstention seems to have been greater in the urban areas than in the rural constituencies, but fairly evenly distributed throughout the United Kingdom. In fact in no constituency did the poll reach 40 per cent, with the Welsh voting more than the Scots, and the latter more than the English. The highest turn-out was in the Highlands and Islands constituency (which elected a SNP representative), the lowest in London North-East, where only 20.4 per cent of electors voted.

Did the size of the poll really come as a surprise? Observers had predicted a low poll, but most of them put it at between 45 and 50 per cent. Yet if one looks back at the opinion polls conducted for the Commission of the European Communities, it is interesting to see that 32 per cent of those questioned in April 1979 said they intended to vote, which is a fairly accurate forecast of the actual poll.

Are there convincing explanations for the abstentions? Firstly, after the general election (which in Scotland and Wales had itself followed a referendum on devolution) a certain degree of weariness and rejection of an additional election probably had some negative effect on the turn-out. Secondly, it is likely that the election of an Assembly whose job is neither to form nor to bring down a Government had little mobilising effect. A kind of negative reaction to a body with so few powers developed all the more easily because there was insufficient knowledge about the European institutions to compensate for it.

Indeed, the lack of information about the Assembly to be elected is the third factor explaining the massive abstentions. An opinion poll conducted by Opinion Research Centre for Independent Television News showed that a third of those interviewed claimed to have abstained because of insufficient information. A fourth factor arises from dislike of the Community, since about a quarter of the people interviewed by ORC claimed to have abstained for this reason. As a result of Labour's confusion about its real intentions with regard to Europe, and its ambiguous position on a possible withdrawal from the Community, the Labour Party did not succeed in mobilising many anti-Marketeers to vote for it.

If it is agreed that, in general, a low poll favours the Conservatives, then this time, with the existing electoral system, it was a decisive factor in their victory, since it is generally estimated that on 10 June two out of every three non-voters normally supported the Labour Party. Of course there were exceptions to this general trend, since a well-known Labour anti-Marketeer — Alf Lomas — was elected with a considerable lead over his Conservative opponent in the London North-East constituency, which had the lowest poll with 79.6 per cent abstaining. Likewise, Wales returned three Labour members to Strasbourg (out of its four Euro-deputies) with a higher average poll in these constituencies than in the rest of Britain.

The results[2]

Italy

In general, the European elections confirmed the changes which took place on 3 June at the time of the legislative elections in Italy: losses by the two major parties, the Christian Democrats and the Communist Party, a modest increase in the Socialists' votes, a clear increase in support for the Liberals, losses for the Republicans, gains for the Radicals, and no change for the extreme Right. But although the trend was the same, with parties which lost votes on 3 June continuing to lose them on 10 June, and those who increased their support continuing to gain votes, the significance of the gains and losses is different in the two elections, and it is here that one is able to discern the distinctiveness of the European vote.

Italy

Parties	Change 10 June 3 June	European elections 10 June 1979			Legislative elections (Chamber) 3 June 1979		
		Votes	Per cent	Seats	Votes	Per cent	Seats
DC	−1.8	12,752,602	36.5	30	14,007,594	38.3	262
PCI	−0.8	10,343,101	29.6	24	11,107,883	30.4	201
PSI	+1.2	3,857,436	11.0	9	3,586,256	9.8	62
PSDI	+0.5	1,511,320	4.3	4	1,403,873	3.8	20
PRI	−0.4	895,083	2.6	2	1,106,766	3.0	16
PLI	+1.7	1,269,560	3.6	3	708,022	1.9	9
PR	+0.3	1,282,728	3.7	3	1,259,362	3.4	18
PDUP	−0.3	404,794	1.1	1	501,431	1.4	6
DP[a]	−0.1	250,414	0.7	1	293,443	0.8	−
MSI	+0.1	1,907,452	5.4	4	1,924,251	5.3	30
DEM NAZ .	−0.2	141,350	0.4	−	228,340	0.6	−
UV[b]	+0.4	165,254	0.5	−	33,250	0.1	1
SVP[c]	−	196,189	0.6	−	206,264	0.6	4

[a] The votes gained by the NSU (Nuova sinistra unita) have been included in the DP list for the legislative elections on 3 June.
[b] The Union Valdotaine includes the autonomist movements.
[c] The SVP (Süd Tyroler Volkspartei) only stood in the North-East electoral district.

---

[2] For an initial analysis of the results of the European elections, see the 'Dossier des élections européennes' published by the *Revue politique et parlementaire*, July-August 1979, pp. 8-60.

In the legislative elections, the PCI seemed to be the main loser (-4 points) as against the slight decrease in support for the Christian Democrats (-0.4). The winner, despite its limited support, was the Radical Party which showed the highest rate of increase, and which in absolute terms doubled its votes, while the Socialist Party's position remained unchanged.

In the European elections, the DC sustained the most serious losses (down 1.8) while the PCI managed to keep its losses below one point. The two Socialist parties achieved a respectable result, but the most striking result was the outstanding performance of the small Liberal Party which achieved on 10 June what the Radicals had done on 3 June, a doubling of its votes.

Thus what had been forecast in fact came about: the European elections detached the voters from their narrow party allegiances. The PCI did not conform to this rule, however. Despite the waning of Eurocommunism and the heterogeneity and lack of influence of the Communist group in the European Assembly, the party succeeded on 10 June in keeping its losses down. Most voters who decided not to vote for the PCI seem to have spoilt their papers. Moreover, although the PCI lost a not inconsiderable fraction of its voters, especially amongst the young, to the Radical Party on 3 June, on 10 June it was the Socialist Party which benefited from this swing. The Socialists were pinning their hopes on the European elections. Although they made more headway on 10 June than on the 3rd, this does not entirely justify the faith which the party placed in its association with the major European parties: with 11 per cent of the votes it was still a long way from their position of strength. To its advantage one can note, however, that it was in Italy alone, especially if the PSI and PSDI votes are added together, that socialism achieved any success in the European elections. The European mark of its success is partly to be found in the regional distribution of its gains between the two elections in the 'white' regions and in Lombardy (due also to the personal success of Craxi who led the list in Milan), while its lowest percentages were in the South, where it was competing with the Radicals.

The Radical Party, which was the star of the legislative elections, did not maintain its progress in the European elections. Its geographical distribution is highly significant: in comparison with 3 June it lost votes throughout the whole of the North of Italy except in Trentino and Friuli, where it gained some of the 'autonomist' votes. The Radical Party is seen as an element of protest at national level, but part of the electorate which it won over on 3 June did not regard it as sufficiently 'responsible' at European level. In the South, on the other hand, where the protest vote persisted in the European elections, the Radical Party maintained its progress in all areas, with a 1 per cent peak in Sicily and Sardinia.

Although they held some reliable European trump cards, the Christian Democrats lost the most support. In Strasbourg, it is true, they no longer fulfil the two essential functions — as a bulwark against Communism and as main distributor of resources — which in Italy win them the votes of electors whose principal concern is to cast an effective vote. It is interesting, too, to note that the break introduced by the European elections produced two different types of behaviour. In the industrial North, and especially in the big towns, Turin and Milan, the Christian Democrat losses were matched by a marked increase in support for the Liberals (PLI). In this part of Italy, the liberal and secular middle class, which in legislative elections votes for the Christian Democrats because of their anticommunism, voted in the European election for the party closest to the political groups which, in Europe, represent the same socio-economic groups and the same cultural values. In the southern half of the country, however, the Christian Democrats' set-back was in keeping with the general rise of the neo-fascist party, the MSI, much more than with the rise of the Liberal Party, which only attracted a tiny fringe of the electorate. In the first instance, the dynamics of the election brought Italy's situation more in line with the positions of its partners in the EEC, and in the second, it enhanced Italian distinctiveness. It would nevertheless be difficult to explain this phenomenon merely in terms of a greater commitment to Europe on the part of the northern electorate. More likely, freed from the Christian Democrat/PCI bi-polarisation by the special nature of the election, the voters adopted the voting behaviour which is most natural for them.

Germany

In Germany, by gaining three more seats than the SPD-FDP coalition, the CDU-CSU provided the second surprise of the elections. It was expected to form the largest German political group, but it was not generally expected that it would overtake the coalition. By this standard, the 10 June elections closed with the victory of the CDU-CSU.

The SPD obtained 40.8 per cent of the votes, and 34 seats, including one for Berlin. It suffered both from the low poll and from the presence of the 'green' (ecologists) lists. Despite this, one cannot ignore the fact that it was unable to mobilise its own supporters (especially in the Ruhr) and that its trade union candidates got little support from the workers. By gaining only 6 per cent of the votes and 4 seats, the FDP once again found itself in the dangerous 5 per cent area. It explained its poor performance by the fact that its supporters tend to vote only in federal and regional elections, and that its president, Hans-Dietrich Genscher, was not even on his party's list. The explanations of the SPD and the FDP are in fact worth taking into consideration: they show that the European elections cannot be used as a test for a national legislative election. On 10 June municipal elections also took place in two Länder and resulted in gains for the SPD (+6.7 per cent in the Rhineland-Palatinate, +7.4 per cent in the Saar) and losses for the CDU (−4.1 per cent and −4.6 per cent); the FDP also lost support in the two Länder (−1.8 per cent and −0.3 per cent). These results moderate the hasty conclusions which one might draw from 10 June.

The CDU-CSU success came as a surprise, as the parties had had mediocre results in the regional elections since 1978, and it was believed that electors would be put off by the interminable squabbling between the CDU and the CSU, and the constant challenges to the CDU president, Helmut Kohl. Some observers saw the majority vote in favour of the CDU-CSU as proof of the consolidation of democracy in Germany, with citizens voting for parties rather than for personalities. The CDU obtained 39.1 per cent of the votes and 32 seats including two for Berlin, and the CSU 10.1 per cent and eight seats. In percentage of votes, the CSU obtained 60 per cent of the Bavarian votes in the 1976 federal elections and 62.5 per cent on

Federal Republic of Germany

	10 June 1979 European election			3 October 1976 Federal election		
		Per cent	Seats		Per cent	Seats
Electorate	42,700,919			42,058,015		
Votes cast	28,119,532	65.9		38,165,753	90.7	
Spoilt papers . . .	255,775	0.9		343,253	0.9	
Valid votes cast .	27,863,757	99.1	78*	37,882,500	99.1	496
SPD	11,377,818	40.8	34	16,099,019	42.6	214
CDU	10,890,955	39.1	32	14,367,302	38.0	190
CSU	2,816,758	10.1	8	4,027,499	10.6	53
FDP	1,663,506	6.0	4	2,995,085	7.9	39
DKP	112,184	0.4	–	118,581	0.3	–
EAP	31,847	0.1	–	6,811	0.0	–
CBV	45,308	0.2		6,720	0.0	–
Zentrum	31,871	0.1	–	–	–	–
Greens/Grünen . .	893,510	3.2	–	–	–	–

* Plus three deputies for West Berlin selected by the West Berlin Chamber of Deputies

10 June; but in 1976 it obtained more than 4 million votes, whereas in 1979 it only reached 2.8 million votes, so that, calculating at federal level, the CSU's share dropped from 10.6 to 10.1 per cent. The winning party was incontestably the CDU, especially in North Rhine-Westphalia, where the poll was higher than in the other Länder (+1.3 per cent) in comparison with 1976, with the SPD losing by –2.6 per cent. These indicators attracted the more attention because, in this very important Land, the regional elections will take place in Spring 1980, before the federal elections in the Autumn.[3]

According to an analysis of the results published by INFAS (*Süddeutsche Zeitung*, 12 June), the point of comparison for the European elections should be not the federal but the regional elections (less at stake, lower poll). By generalising the regional election results since 1978 one obtains figures which are almost identical to those for the European elections, with merely a slight difference for the CDU-CSU (49.6 per cent in the regional elections, 49.2 per cent in the European elections); SPD (40.8 per cent in both cases); FDP (6 per cent in both cases); others (3.6 per cent in both cases). According to INFAS the European elections mobilised the elements which are most loyal to the parties, those who were eager to prove their loyalty, since nothing could change their vote. The results of 10 June expressed the great stability of the party system, and a balance between the majority and the

---

[3]The results of the election in North Rhine-Westphalia in 1980 were: SPD – 106 seats (48.4%); CDU – 95 seats (43.2%); and FDP – 0 seats (4.98%). As the FDP obtained less than 5% of the vote, they did not obtain any seats in the Lander parliament.

opposition. The SPD-FDP coalition won in the 1976 federal elections with 2 points more than the CDU-CSU; their relationship was reversed in the European election. Few regional variations stand out in this election. It should be noted, however, that the CDU gained most votes in Schleswig-Holstein (+3.7 per cent) where its results had been poor in 1976. The case of the Ruhr has already been mentioned. Because the European and the municipal elections fell on the same day, there was a much higher poll in Rhineland-Palatinate (77 per cent) and in the Saar (83 per cent) than in the rest of the federal territory (65.9 per cent). One can conclude from this that the municipal elections motivated electors to vote more than the European ones.

The small parties obtained only 3.6 per cent of the votes. The 'green' parties had several spectacular results in Bremen and Baden-Württemberg (nearly 5 per cent).

France

In France, if one compares the results, with respect to the registered electorate, of the 10 June 1979 election with the results of the March 1978 legislative elections, one can discern a dual development of unequal magnitude: the reconversion of the governing coalition's electorate in favour of the Giscardians, and the consolidation of the Left's electorate, in which the trend towards a redistribution in favour of the Socialist Party which began in 1973 was halted. But, overall, the balance between forces of the Left and forces of the Right was scarcely altered.

The massive shift of RPR voters to the UDF was a bitter blow for the Gaullists. They gained only 16.24 per cent of votes cast, as opposed to 22.62 per cent in the legislative elections. Only 9.35 per cent of the electorate voted for them. Not only was the violently anti-Giscardian campaign unsuccessful at national level — the RPR suffered losses throughout the whole country except in Corsica — but at regional level the anti-European campaign in the areas most directly affected by Community policy did not produce the benefits which were expected. Neither in Languedoc-Roussillon (-2.72) nor in the Midi-Pyrénées (-5.89) did the campaign against enlargement of the Common Market benefit the RPR: it lost support in ten out of thirteen départements (the exceptions were Lozère, Aveyron and Gers). For their part neither the people in Alsace nor those in Lorraine seem to have appreciated the aggressive and ultra-nationalist campaign led by Messrs Debré and Chirac. In its 'fief' in Alsace the RPR was overtaken by the UDF and by the PS; it lost twenty points in relation to the 1978 legislative elections in Lower-Rhine (Strasbourg and the surrounding area). In Lorraine, the RPR experienced a serious setback in the steel-producing area (losing 6 points in Moselle) and also in the Vosges, a traditional bastion of Gaullism (where it lost 12 points). While the RPR lost a lot of ground in nineteen of the twenty-two regions in France (it gained 0.13 in Corsica and lost less than one point in Auvergne and Lower Normandy), the UDF increased its support in twenty regions (Lower Normandy: -4.84 and Auvergne: -0.40 were the exceptions), including the regions especially affected by the crisis, by industrial re-structuring or by unemployment. The results in the Nord-Pas-de-Calais and in Provence-Côte d'Azur, in the Pays de la Loire and in many other areas, including Lorraine, confirm the spectacular reversal of forces in the governing parties in favour of the Presidential party.

France: Final results[4]

Electorate: 35,180,531
Votes cast: 21,356,960
Abstentions: 18,823,571 (39.29 per cent)
Spoilt papers: 1,114,613 (3.16 per cent[a]; 5.21 per cent[b])
Valid votes cast: 20,242,347

	Valid votes cast	Per cent	Seats
Extreme left Trotskyist (Mme Laguiller) . . .	623,663	3.08	
PCF (Marchais)	4,153,710	20.52	19
PS and MRG (Mitterrand)	4,763,026	23.53	22
RPR (Chirac)	3,301,980	16.31	15
UDF (Mme Veil)	5,588,851	27.61	25
Ecologists (Mme Fernex)	888,134	4.39	
Employment-Equality-Europe (Servan-Schreiber)	373,259	1.84	
Défense interprofessionnelle (Malaud)	283,144	1.40	
Eurodroite (Tixier-Vignancour)	265,911	1.31	
Régions-Europe (Hallier)	337	0	
PSU (Mme Bouchardeau)	332	0	

[a] per cent of electorate
[b] percent of votes cast

The moderate and rather hazy campaign conducted by the Socialist Party was not enough to win the support of its potential electors (4 or 5 per cent of the electorate): the PS did not succeed in capturing this electorate, which is hesitant, unstable, attracted as much by the Left as by the Right, captivated by the arguments of the ecologists and tempted to abstain. For the first time since 1973 the Socialist Party did not increase its support. As a result, the gap separating the PCF from the PS and the MRG was slightly reduced (3 points instead of 4.15). In

[4]The results of the election were published by the Ministry of the Interior in the evening of 13 June. Arguing that a large number of voters had used Mme Veil's 'policy statements' rather than the normal voting papers in casting their votes, which had thus been invalid, Mme Veil's supporters demanded a recount at the departmental commissions. Thus the official results were not broadcast until ten days after the election (on 20 June at 18.00 hours). The national committee in charge of counting the votes declared that the circulars and policy statements distributed by the lists could be regarded as valid votes provided that they bore the title of the list and the names of the 81 candidates in the order in which they were nominated'. As a result, 108,309 votes counted as spoilt papers on 13 June were considered valid on the 20th. The main beneficiary of this decision, Mme Veil's list, was credited with 78,958 new votes and an additional seat in Strasbourg, to the detriment of the PS-MRG list which lost 1,315 votes and its twenty-second representative in the European Assembly. On 22 October 1979 the Conseil d'Etat reversed this decision. It returned to the Socialist Party the seat which had been taken from it, and reduced from 26 to 25 the number of seats allocated to the list led by Mme Veil.

twenty-eight départements, as opposed to twenty-four, the Communists came ahead of the Socialists and the left-wing Radicals.

The campaign which the PCF conducted on specifically European issues in the wine-growing regions and in the steel-producing area produced uneven results. A campaign which centred on opposition to the enlargement of the Common Market to include Greece, Spain and Portugal enabled them to record some general progress in Languedoc-Roussillon (+1.54 per cent) and in Midi-Pyrénées (+1.62 per cent). In the former, the success was greater and was achieved in Hérault thanks to the inclusion of Maffre-Baugé in the Communist list. The PCF gained 4.52 points and snatched first place from the PS, which lost 4.48. Elsewhere, in several départements which are subject to competition from Spain and Portugal, the PCF's position remained unchanged (Eastern Pyrénées, Gard) or advanced in the same — meagre — proportion as the PS (Aude). In the Midi-Pyrénées region where the PS deputies are in the majority and there are no Communist deputies, the PCF increased its support in almost all the départements (except Ariège and Tarn-et-Garonne) by one or two points, while the PS lost support in eight départements in the region.

From these results it looks as if the campaign against the enlargement of the Common Market, which did the RPR no good, gained the PCF some votes at the expense of the Socialist Party. Though satisfactory, the results in the South-West were not spectacular, however. They were still uneven, and there was a high percentage of abstentions in the thirteeen départements in the South-West which are close to Spain: in Hérault they reached 41.03 per cent and in the Eastern Pyrénées 43.28 per cent.

In the East, where the steelmen's battles were compared with a battle for national liberation, the ultra-nationalistic campaign was not wholly successful. The PCF experienced a set-back in Alsace (−0.43) and an even greater one in Lorraine. In this region, where the UDF made some slight progress (+1.22) but where the other three parties lost ground, the PCF suffered from the lowest turn-out, in the steel-producing area (45.55 per cent in Moselle) including the working-class electorate, and from the break-through by the extreme Left. The high point of its campaign was a meeting in Longwy presided over by Georges Marchais, which attracted about 10,000 people. It produced positive results locally: the PCF gained between 50 and 60 per cent of the votes in some of the small communes which are directly affected by the dismantling of the steel industry. In general, however, the results were uneven, and the PCF suffered some serious losses in several large municipalities led by Communist mayors. In other crisis-ridden industrial regions, notably the Nord-Pas-de-Calais, where the Communists conducted a very lively campaign, the PCF no more than held its own, and even suffered some losses, as in the steel-producing area of Valenciennois, where a huge campaign had been mounted. But in this area, Pierre Mauroy's stronghold and a bastion of the Socialists, it gave the PCF great satisfaction to come ahead of the Socialist Party.

In general, the PCF's success seems to have been a success by default: the party did not lose ground, but it gained the votes of only 11.84 per cent of the whole electorate, and remained in a mediocre position in relation to the votes cast. As soon as the first results were analysed, *l'Humanité* (12 June) drew attention to the PCF's set-backs in the urban districts, explaining this by a low poll amongst Communist voters, especially in the working-class areas. In general, the PCF made its progress in the rural areas, whilst its share of the vote remained constant or from time to time decreased in the industrial areas. In these areas, the young workers tended to vote for the extreme Left or for the ecologists, to the detriment of the Communist Party.

United Kingdom
As for the United Kingdom, the results in the following table demonstrate the resounding victory of the Conservatives. By winning 60 of the 78 seats at stake, they confined the Labour successes to Western Scotland, the North of England, South Wales and, to a lesser extent, London (where Labour won 2 of the 10 seats).

United Kingdom

Poll: 33.0 per cent

	Votes cast	Per cent	Seats
Conservatives	6,508,481	48.4	60
Labour Party	4,393,832	32.7	18
Liberals	1,690,600	12.6	—
Others	853,249	5.7	3
Total	13,446,162		81

Great Britain

Poll: 32.6 per cent

	Votes cast	Per cent	Seats
Conservatives	6,508,481	50.6	60
Labour Party	4,253,210	33.0	17
Liberals	1,690,600	13.1	—
SNP	247,836	1.9	1
Total	12,700,127		78

Northern Ireland

Poll: 57.0 per cent

	Votes cast	Per cent	Seats
Democratic Unionists	170,688	45.0	1
Social Democratic and Labour Party	140,622	37.1	1
Official Unionists	68,185	17.9	1
Total	379,495		3

The Liberals, who, with 13 per cent of the votes, are not represented in Strasbourg as a result of their scattered electorate, were the big losers in the election although their best-placed candidate, Russell Johnston, was narrowly beaten by the SNP candidate, and although they were in second place in nine constituencies (as a comparison, in the general election of 3 May, with 13.8 per cent of the votes, they obtained 11 seats). On the other hand, the Scottish National Party, by returning Mrs Ewing, a member of the previous European Assembly, to Strasbourg, softened the blow of its defeat in the legislative elections, when it lost nine of the eleven seats it held previously. Northern Ireland elected three Euro-deputies: a Catholic member of the Social Democratic and Labour Party, John Hume, who would be a member of the Labour Party delegation in Strasbourg, an official Unionist, John Taylor, and a well-known figure in Irish politics, the Rev. Ian Paisley, as a Democratic Unionist (the last two can hardly be counted amongst the pro-Europeans).

The percentage of votes gained by the political parties in comparison with the general election indicated an average swing to the Conservatives of nearly 5 per cent. As the Liberals just about retained their position, the swing was basically away from Labour. Had it gained the same percentage of votes as it had on 3 May, the Labour Party would have gained 29 seats against the Conservatives' 49. But the swing is not enough to explain such a spectacular Conservative victory. The electoral system had a lot to do with it, since it produced a strong disproportion between votes won and seats allocated. With 33 per cent of the votes, Labour gained only 17 seats, whereas 50 per cent of the votes gave the Conservatives 60 seats, and the Liberals, with 13 per cent, got none at all. According to the calculations which have been made, with a system of proportional representation, and with the same number of votes, the results would have been: 39 seats to the Conservatives, 26 to Labour, 10 to the Liberals.

Furthermore, the size of the constituencies seems to have magnified the advantages of the electoral system to the Conservatives' benefit, since the grouping of urban parliamentary constituencies (which normally support Labour) had the effect of concentrating Labour's electorate on a small number of Euro-candidates.

But although it is indisputable that the electoral system reinforced the advantage gained by the Conservatives, one should not under-estimate the impact of a campaign prepared well in advance and which reflected the relative harmony of views on Europe within the party. The Labour Party, on the other hand, with its internal divisions and an unconvincing campaign, was unable to mobilise the dissatisfaction of public opinion which is nevertheless disposed — as all the opinion polls confirm — to blame the EEC for many of the United Kingdom's ills.

Be that as it may, although the Conservative victory can be understood as part of the shift to the Right which had already appeared in the general election and which was then spurred on by a kind of dynamic of success, it is difficult to see in this — taking account of the high level of abstentions — any decisive advance for the most enthusiastic pro-Marketeers, for the British clearly remain unwilling Europeans. The preparations, the events, and the results of the European election showed that, after more than five years' membership of the EEC, the United Kingdom is not a European country like the others. Consequently one may wonder how the British political parties envisage transnational co-operation in the European Assembly.

The atmosphere in the Socialist group in Strasbourg is likely to be affected by the campaign which the Labour Party conducted and by the results of the election. Held responsible both for the relative decline of the Socialist group and for the advance made by the Right in the new Assembly, the British are already under fire from certain Socialist leaders in Europe (like Claude Cheysson). With a delegation which includes six active anti-Marketeers and a dozen Euro-deputies half of whom are determined 'reformists' and half pro-Marketeers, what kind of co-operation can be envisaged? Will a little European 'socialisation' bring Labour to co-operate more with its 'sister' parties, or will there, on the other hand, be a nationalist backlash?

The Conservatives, however, appear to be willing to co-operate, as was already shown by their membership of the European Democratic Union, which Mrs Thatcher sees as preparing the way for a grand alliance of the Centre-Right, based on a rapprochement between Conservatives and Christian Democrats. It was no doubt to disarm the hostility of the Italian and Dutch Christian Democrats — who, unlike the CDU-CSU, are not all in favour of such an alliance — that the British Conservatives in Strasbourg have taken the title of 'European Democrat group' hoping thus to rid themselves of the negative connotations which the word 'conservative' has in Europe.

V Conclusion

The diagram indicates the distribution of the new members by political groups, and shows, as was emphasised by the initial observers, a certain shift to the Right in comparison with the previous Assembly. Although the Socialists remain the most important group in numerical terms, the Left is politically in a minority vis à vis the predictable alliance between the Right and the Centre. Despite the adoption of proportional representation by all the countries except Britain, the major parties dominate the Assembly.

Composition of the new European Assembly

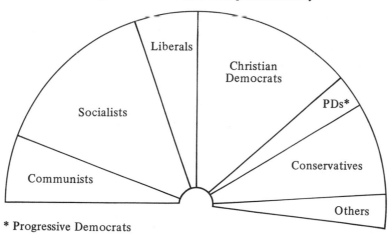

* Progressive Democrats

The small parties were crushed in the European election mainly because of the retention of a majority voting system in the United Kingdom, and the restrictions imposed on the internal functioning of proportional representation in France and West Germany. Except in Italy, where 19 Euro-deputies belong to parties which obtained less than 6 per cent of the votes, the small parties were conspicuously disadvantaged. The most remarkable example is the complete absence from Strasbourg of any representative of the British Liberal Party, which is nevertheless the most European of the parties in Britain, and which had obtained 13 per cent of the votes. In France, with a different electoral system, the small parties, which were disadvantaged by the 5 per cent rule and under serious financial constraints, have no seats in the European Assembly, although they obtained nearly 12 per cent of the votes cast.

Moreover, the domestication of the issues, the traditional aspect of the election, and the predominance of the major parties probably discouraged those who would prefer a Europe of citizens to a Europe of political parties and nation-States. Nowhere did political movements such as the regionalists and the ecologists have the opportunity, as they could legitimately have hoped to have, to express a political philosophy which recognises no frontiers.

Following its direct election the new Parliament will find itself confronted with a dual logic: on the one side, reinforcing its powers, on account of its new popular legitimacy and its greater numbers (it went up from 198 to 410 members); on the other, the weight of national demands such as those which were expressed during the election campaign. The former will probably lead, if not to a demand for greater powers, at least to a more systematic use of those which it possesses. It is obvious that, even without legislative power, the obstinate use of its powers concerning the Budget and the control of the Commission could constitute a considerable means by which the Parliament could exert pressure. The more so as the members are likely to undergo a process of European 'socialisation', which will bring out a new 'loyalty' born of membership of an instituion which is *sui generis*. At a time when the prospect of enlarging the EEC is arousing new thoughts about its institutional workings (the Three Wise Men's report, the Spierenburg report), the way in which the newly-elected Parliament will assert itself is as important as it is unpredictable.

However, the European logic cannot triumph totally over the national preoccupations which as we have seen, dominated this election. It should not be forgotten that many members (notably the French Communists, the DIFE list, and the British Labour Party) were elected to block all developments towards any form of supranationalism whatsoever, and that all of them were competing with each other to assure the electors that their party would be the best defender of national interests in Strasbourg. In addition, election by universal suffrage will inevitably make members of the European Parliament more attentive to local and sectoral interests, the protection of which will weigh upon their re-election.

The multiple combinations of these variables further complicate a parliamentary system which has no pre-existing model as a reference point. In fact, the different European political groups cannot be compared with true political parties, for the potential inter-party alliances which the election campaigns revealed represent centrifugal forces threatening party cohesion. One can all the more easily imagine that the groups will divide and re-form according to ideological, political and national imperatives, since the members of the European Parliament are not accustomed to dealing with European issues, which are after all highly technical.

Finally, a number of practical problems complicate the Euro-deputy's task, and at first threaten to divert his energies towards problems of secondary importance:

the old rules which are ill-adjusted to the workings of the new Assembly, the co-existence of six official languages, and the absence of a permanent headquarters will facilitate neither the progress of parliamentary business nor the apprenticeship of novices. Apart from this, the members of the European Parliament will have to work out satisfactory arrangements with the national parliamentary groups, their parties' leaderships and their electorates.[1]

In this intermediate period it is likely that procedural debates will prevail over discussions about fundamental issues, and that a period of adaptation will be needed before the major guidelines upon which a real European political system will be based can develop. Such a system will only emerge if the European Parliament functions coherently and if stable majorities develop to deal with the fundamental problems confronting the Community. Above all, the three institutions of the Community must somehow learn to live together by pragmatically establishing an allocation of roles which encourages both criticism and the discussion of new ideas.

---

[1] For a more detailed discussion see David Coombes, *The Future of the European Parliament,* PSI/European Centre for Political Studies, Studies in European Politics 1, 1979.

The POLICY STUDIES INSTITUTE (PSI) is a British independent policy research organisation concerned with issues relevant to economic and social policies and the working of political institutions.

PSI was formed in April 1978 through the merger of Political and Economic Planning (PEP), founded in 1931, and the Centre for Studies in Social Policy (CSSP), founded in 1972. It continues the tradition of both organisations to establish the facts by impartial empirical research and to relate the findings to practical policy making. The scope of the Institute's work has been extended by the recent establishment of a European Centre for Political Studies. PSI's work is financed by grants for specific studies made by trusts, foundations and public bodies, with substantial support from donations by industry and commerce, and by annual subscriptions.

The results of the studies are disseminated widely by means of frequent publications, articles and seminars.

1-2 Castle Lane, London SW1E 6DR
Telephone: 01-828 7075

How to obtain PSI publications

PSI publications may be obtained from booksellers or direct from PSI. Postage and packing will be additional to the cost of the publication if it is sent by post.

A full list of recent publications and subscription details will be sent on request to PSI at 1-2 Castle Lane, London SW1E 6DR.

Already published

Reports

No. 574	Ulster Today and Tomorrow (1978)	Price £3.20
No. 575	Training Adults for Skilled Jobs (1978)	Price £4.80
No. 576	Creating New Jobs: a report on long term job creation in Britain and Sweden (1978)	Price £3.60
No. 577	The Impact of Employment Protection Laws (1978)	Price £3.80
No. 578	Private and National Health Services (1978)	Price £2.20
No. 579	Westminster and Devolution (1978)	Price £1.80
No. 580	The Management of Public Expenditure (1979)	Price £3.50
No. 581	Independent Further Education (1979)	Price £4.50
No. 582	Unemployed Professional Executives (1979)	Price £4.75
No. 589	Walking *is* Transport (1979)	Price £3.50
No. 584	Swings for the Schools (1979)	Price £1.00
No. 585	Japanese Industrial Policy (1980)	Price £3.95
No. 586	Differentials for Managers and Skilled Manual Workers in the United Kingdom (1980)	Price £3.95
No. 587	The Social Consequences of Rail Closures (1980)	Price £4.50
No. 588	Maternity Rights (1980)	Price £4.95

Studies in European Politics

1.	The Future of the European Parliament (1979)	Price £3.95
2.	Towards Transnational Parties in the European Community (1979)	Price £1.80
3.	European Integration, Regional Devolution and National Parliaments (1979)	Price £2.25
4.	Eurocommunism and Foreign Policy (1979)	Price £2.95

Discussion Papers

No. 1	Discussing the Welfare State (1980)	Price £2.75
No. 2	The Welfare State – Diversity and Decentralisation (1980)	Price £2.75
No. 3	Public Policy and Family Life (1980)	Price £2.75